MARYLAND'S EASTERN SHORE

A Guide for Wanderers

MARYLAND'S EASTERN SHORE

A Guide for Wanderers

MARY U. CORDDRY

Literary House Press
Washington College
Chestertown, Maryland

*To the memory of
James G. Nelson,
whose friendship and loyalty
to Washington College,
the Literary House Press, and the author
gave this book its origins.*

The Literary House Press
at Washington College
Chestertown, Maryland 21620-1681

Library of Congress Catalog Card Number
97-071909

ISBN 0-937692-14-X

Printed in the United States of America

Publisher's Note:
Since many of the community museums and historic
structures listed depend on volunteers for their
existence and openings, and are maintained by
organizations with changing leadership, the hours
and contact telephone numbers may not always hold
up. In such cases, access may depend on personal
initiative.

CONTENTS

INTRODUCTION

*T*here are two kinds of visitor to the Eastern Shore—the destination traveler and the meanderer. The destination traveler swoops along U.S. 50 from the west or down U.S. 13 from the north, to a specific terminus that is probably Ocean City. The meanderer comes to explore what is in between. He creates his own diversion by driving off the main highways through forests, marshes, soybean fields, and isolated villages and finding unexpected adventure.

It is hoped that this will be a meanderer's guide to the pleasures of simple discovery.

The Eastern Shore of Maryland is, by geography and mystique, a place apart. Its attraction lies in being close to home but not like home. Because it is on a peninsula between Chesapeake Bay and the Atlantic Ocean, the teeming megalopolis and aggressive traffic between New York and Washington, D.C. passed it by to the west. It was all but overlooked.

It remained a rural area, an island of darkness when viewed from above from a plane at night. Its people retained their own distinctive accent and figures of speech and were about a year behind in prevailing fashion. The region's background and character remained as English as in its earliest years of settlement. There was little overlap between the dominant white society and the separate communities, schools, churches, and culture of its black population.It is only in recent years that its black leaders have become politically active and increasingly sophisticated and that its population has begun to reflect the cultural mix that prevails only an hour or two away by car in Washington or Baltimore.

In 1952 the first span of the Chesapeake Bay Bridge replaced the ferry system that had, up to that time, been the only east-west link between the Eastern Shore and the rest of Maryland. What seemed to be at least half the population west of the bay immediately headed for the ocean beaches. Backups of traffic on both sides of the bridge became the subject of Monday morning horror stories after summer weekends. A second span was completed in 1973.

From the first it has been more than traffic that has crossed the bridge in relentless flow. It has been suburbia.

In spite of new construction, a changing population, environmental controversy, zoning battles, Wal-Marts, fast food chains, shopping malls bigger than whole downtown areas, and the intensive economic development efforts of business organizations, Washington and Baltimore newspapers continue to view "the Shore" as a region of watermen, eccentric characters, and "sleepy little towns." The Shore is seldom separated from stock phrases such as "changeless," or "frozen-in-time."

That is the mystique. That is what feature writers, photographers, and artists (amateur and professional), seekers of retirement havens, and visitors who may be reading this guide are looking for. And that is what, in spite of everything, the Shore still has to offer, if the visitor knows how to look for it.

To approach the Shore correctly the visitor must first cast off the image stubbornly held by outsiders of "The Shore" as a single entity. The Shore is, after all, the designation for nine counties and encompasses thirty-six percent of Maryland's total land area. It can be divided into segments as distinct from each other as the region itself is from the rest of the state. The divisions go beyond geography to basic character.

Politically the Shore is viewed, correctly, as one of the most conservative areas in the United States. There are, however, two brands of conservatism here as distinct from each other as the areas that foster them. On the Upper Shore it is a conservatism that resists change. On the Lower Shore it is a conservatism that defends, vehemently, the rights of the private property owner to do what he wants with his land, and that includes development.

The difference could be that the "good life" on the Upper Shore is symbolized by secluded estates and historic waterfront villages, and on the Lower Shore by the sleek new condominiums of Ocean City and contemporary homes on once marginal land along its rivers.

In the Lower Shore counties of Somerset, Worcester, Wicomico, and Dorchester south of the Choptank River, elevations are so low that the rivers that empty into Tangier Sound and hence into Chesapeake Bay, merge into vast expanses of marshlands, designated in recent years as wetlands crucial to the ecological balance of natural and human life. On the ocean side, the lowlands are protected from the waves of the Atlantic only by the narrow strip of barrier islands that are Ocean City and Assateague National Seashore.

In the Upper Shore counties of Talbot, Queen Anne's, Kent, Cecil, and the only inland county, Caroline, elevations rise one hundred feet and more. From some of its beautiful unspoiled fields and woods one can gaze from high banks onto the bay's shipping channel from Baltimore to the Chesapeake and Delaware Canal.

To divide the Shore into parts, or, more precisely, layers, the first could be called Avalon, or The Land of Pleasant Living. This side of the region's character is concentrated on the Upper Shore where admirals, generals, chairmen of the board, and executives of some of the nation's major corporations have come, not after death as King Arthur, but to retire. Here they have found the ultimate luxuries—seclusion and waterfronts—on historic estates only a few hours away from the major cities of the East Coast.

Others of the affluent from elsewhere have changed the character of towns such as Oxford and St. Michaels, buying homes once occupied by watermen at prices that have become astounding.

The second Shore, overlapping and merging with the first, could be defined as the Native Shore of the farmer and the waterman. The watermen, diminishing but still significant, personify the Shore that both the estate owner and the visitor want to preserve. The skipjack under sail, the crab feast, the oyster tonger, are the emblems of Maryland, but the waterman today is more likely to stay afloat by taking pleasure passengers or fishing parties on the water than harvesting the bay.

The third Shore, not at all part of the mystique, but part of the future, is the Progressive Shore. This is the Shore of the Salisbury area where civic-minded business leaders have worked diligently to attract industry, develop a first-class hospital, and create a thriving regional metropolis. Scores of spacious and elegant new homes along the Wicomico River or in subdivisions around the city's rim attest to their success. They also demonstrate the changing tastes in a town where less than twenty years ago, the standard style for architecture and decorative arts was colonial, and the only contemporary art and decor to be seen anywhere around were in the new condominiums rising on the Ocean City beaches.

Scattered through all these regions within a region is still another Shore, reflecting the character of none of the others but creating one all its own. It is a kind of decentralized colony of artists, potters, musicians, and intellectuals who acquire and fix up old gabled houses on isolated waterfronts still undiscovered by more affluent seekers of the good life. On the Lower Shore, many of these newcomers connect with the University of Maryland Eastern Shore in Princess Anne or with Salisbury State University. On the Upper Shore, they become part of the full and active program of Easton's Academy of the Arts, and in Chestertown, enjoy the proximity of Washington College.

On all parts of the Shore, they bring new excitement to a natural setting and historic background dismissed or taken for granted by lifelong residents.

This guide is intended to direct the visitor to the new or enlivened local museums and historic churches that are part of this new awareness. For the meanderer, it provides destinations. The destinations are rewarding in themselves, but the user might also discover that getting there, over some of the less traveled byways of the Shore, is an adventure in itself.

Scattered throughout the Eastern Shore are small rural churches, beautiful in their simplicity and remarkable in their little-noted significance in the history of this nation.

The American roots of five major denominations—Methodist, Presbyterian, Quaker, Episcopalian, and Roman Catholic—are to be found on the peninsula shared by Virginia, Maryland, and Delaware.

Throughout this guide some of the Eastern Shore churches that established these roots will be singled out for the traveler who might otherwise pass by them unaware. Some are still active, some open only for special annual events, and some open not at all.

Even if not open to visitors, they are worth a stop for their simple presence and, in some cases, for cemeteries in which are buried heroes and heroines of our nation's early years.

MARYLAND'S EASTERN SHORE

LOWER SHORE

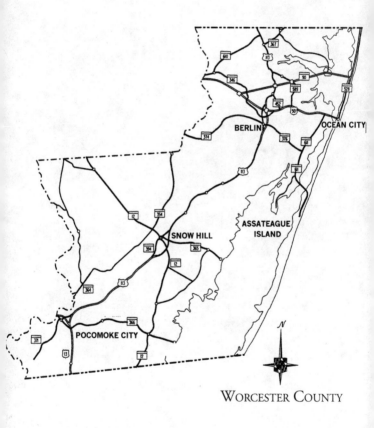

BERLIN

OCEAN CITY

SNOW HILL

ASSATEAGUE
ISLAND

POCOMOKE CITY

N

WORCESTER COUNTY

WORCESTER COUNTY

OCEAN CITY

THE LOWER SHORE'S BEACH-TO-BAY INDIAN TRAIL

At the southernmost tip of Ocean City, a twenty-seven-foot-high Indian head carved of wood looks stolidly across the Inlet toward Assateague Island. This is the starting point of an eighty-two-mile self-guided driving circuit similar to the Indian Trail once used by the Assateagues, Pocomokes, Manikin, Animuses, and Acquinticas tribes of the Algonquin nation that then occupied this land. It has been designated a National Recreation Trail.

The trail leads the adventurous motorist to the historic towns of Berlin and Snow Hill, through the Pocomoke Forest to Princess Anne—a Somerset County town where the past seems to overshadow the present—on to the Chesapeake Bay fishing port of Crisfield, and back through Pocomoke City to the starting point at Ocean City.

The traveler is guided by signs bearing the Maryland emblem with Indian arrowheads pointing to special attractions along the way. The trail leads to small museums and historic sites through farm fields and forests and small rural towns that will be as much a part of this low-key adventure as the listed destinations.

Wanderers are advised to pick up a trail map in Ocean City.

The trail begins with . . .

THE INDIAN HEAD AT OCEAN CITY INLET

In the summer of 1976, Peter Toth, a wandering Hungarian-born artist, then age twenty-seven, came to Ocean City and offered to create as a gift to the resort an outdoor wood sculpture that would be his personal tribute to the American Indian.

The result, carved from an immense log and set in concrete, is the centerpiece of a small park created by the town's Beautification Committee that marks the beginning of the Indian Trail.

The Ocean City sculpture brought the artist halfway to his stated goal, to create as "my gift to America" a monument to the Indian in each of the fifty states. He lived and traveled in a van with a sheepdog named Smoke and supported himself with occasional jobs in machine shops and the sale of small carvings.

Ocean City's Indian Head

By the late 1980s, Peter Toth had completed fifty-eight monuments, one in every state, including one thirty feet tall in Valdez, Alaska. He circulated a brochure explaining his "Trail of the Whispering Giants," and has written a book called *Indian Giver.* He has yet to reach his final goal, an Indian memorial in Washington, D.C., carved from "a gigantic redwood or Sequoia log."

OCEAN CITY LIFE-SAVING STATION MUSEUM

Where: *On the Boardwalk at the Inlet*
When: *Open June through September, 11 a.m. to*
       10 p.m.; May and October, 11 a.m. to 4 p.m.;
       winter weekends, noon to 4 p.m.
Phone: *410-289-4991*
and . . . Entry fee

At the south end of the boardwalk, past the amusement rides, food booths, T-shirt and trinket shops, a life-saving station built in 1891 houses remnants of the resort's past, visible nowhere else today along this overbuilt strip of sand. The old station itself is one of the few from its period remaining on the East Coast.

The early stations were two-story white clapboard structures topped with a small cupola and manned by the United States Life-Saving Service that, in 1914, became the United States Coast Guard. This one was moved to its present site in 1977 through the efforts of the Ocean City Museum Society.

Its engrossing exhibits recall a past when the local watermen who manned the station launched

into stormy seas in open lifeboats (such as the twenty-six-foot one on display) to rescue the crews of ships in distress. The wrecks recalled in these exhibits

A rescued life-saving station dating to 1891 houses relics of Ocean City's past.

include those ships sunk off the resort's coast by German submarines during World War II.

Other exhibits relate to the days when most of the resort's male population made their livings from the sea while their wives were running the first of the old landmark hotels along the original downtown boardwalk. There are models of familiar old hotels and artifacts that make memories more fun than the arcades outside.

VISITOR CENTER
ASSATEAGUE ISLAND NATIONAL SEASHORE

Where: At the Maryland end of the seashore, south of Ocean City on Rt. 611
Phone: 410-641-1441

Before crossing the bridge to the national seashore, the visitor center is worth a stop to see exhibits related to dune and marsh ecology, an aquarium, and mural-sized photographs of the natural life on the island. There is also a bookstore with audio cassette tapes available for an island drive.

The national seashore is managed by the National Park Service and is one of three major public areas on the barrier island. Assateague State Park, also at the northern end, is managed by the

Maryland Department of Natural Resources.
Chincoteague National Wildlife Refuge at the
southern or Virginia end is managed by the United
States Fish and Wildlife Service.

BERLIN

*B*erlin, one of the first permanent settle-
ments in its region, may be overshadowed
but is not overwhelmed by Ocean City and beach
area development.

In the heart of its downtown, the old Atlantic Hotel has been brought to new life in
elegant Victorian style. Beside it, the Globe
Theater has become a gathering place, with a
bookstore, café, art gallery, and coffeehouse-
style entertainment.

Down the street is one of the big achievements
of the Berlin Heritage Foundation, the Calvin B.
Taylor House.

CALVIN B. TAYLOR HOUSE

Where: At the corner of Main Street and Baker Street
When: Open mid-May through September—Monday,
Wednesday, Friday, and Saturday: 1 p.m. to
4 p.m.

Phone: 410-641-1019
and . . . Entry fee

This rambling, white frame, early nineteenth-century house in its wide tree-shaded lawn was rescued by Berlin's mayor and council and the Berlin Heritage Foundation from planned destruction. With contributions from local citizens and the Maryland Historical Trust, extensive termite damage was repaired, windows replaced, and new roofing put on. It is now a house museum containing furnishings of the period and documents and artifacts related to the town's past.

Renovating the house preserves a period in the town during the early 1800s when prospering landed families built big and now-vanishing gable-fronted homes along its quiet streets. The owner of this one was the first principal of Berlin High School, a superintendent of Worcester County schools, a lawyer, member of the Maryland House of Delegates, and founder of a bank bearing his name. The restoration of his house is a symbol of the general revitalization of the town.

SNOW HILL

*T*his pleasant town with lovely old homes set on wide lawns (three of the loveliest now offer bed and breakfast) has been the Worcester county seat since 1742. If the courthouse seems outsized for its small town setting, it must be remembered that it serves not just the farms that surround the town with wide expanses of corn and soybeans, but Ocean City, which becomes in summer Maryland's second biggest city.

Snow Hill, which is named for a section of London, sits beside the Pocomoke River, an Algonquin Indian name. The Pocomoke, bordered by cypress swamps and dotted with the tiny islands formed around cypress knees, was Maryland's first designated Wild and Scenic River. Visitors can explore the river by canoe, for rent from the Pocomoke River Canoe Company near the Route 12 bridge at the north side of town. Phone 410-632-3971.

JULIA A. PURNELL MUSEUM

Where: *At 208 West Market Street*
When: *Open April through October, Monday through*
Friday: 10 a.m. to 4 p.m.; Saturday and
Sunday: 1 p.m. to 4 p.m.
Phone: *410-632-0515*
and . . . Entry fee

This delightful small museum in a former church building developed as a kind of communal attic. The collection was started early in this century by William Z. Purnell, an outgrowth of his lifelong devotion to his mother, for whom the museum is named.

Snow Hill's Julia A. Purnell Museum, housed in a former church, displays the artifacts of a small town's history.

Julia Purnell's life spanned a century, from 1843 to 1943. After she was confined to a wheelchair at the age of eighty-five, her time was given to the needlework she had always enjoyed. She created more than two thousand pieces, many of them given to friends. Many were original designs based on familiar Snow Hill scenes. At the age of ninety-nine, she won the grand award at the prestigious Philadelphia Hobby Show.

Her son started a small museum in his home to display first his mother's needlework and then other household and farm items that she had used during her long lifetime. Friends added to the collection, and the museum grew. At his death, the collection went to the town of Snow Hill and was moved to its present building.

Volunteers and professionals have worked together to reshape the hodgepodge of about two thousand artifacts into separate exhibits, starting with the area's first inhabitants, the Askiminokonson Indians, and continuing into the memories of most of its visitors.

MT. ZION ONE-ROOM SCHOOL

Where: *On Ironshire Street*
When: *Open July and August, Saturday and Sunday:*
       1 p.m. to 4 p.m.; or by request
Phone: *410-632-0669*

The Worcester County Teachers Association maintains this little school as a museum and opens it for special occasions, sometimes complete with a schoolmarm in costume.

Former students and teachers have helped the association refurbish it and furnish it with a recitation bench, desks, pot-belly stove, bucket and dipper, and old school books to re-create the school days of the past.

ALL HALLOWS EPISCOPAL CHURCH

All Hallows was built in 1748 on a high knoll overlooking what was then a busy avenue of commerce, the Pocomoke River. Its distinctive windows rise to the eaves. In the churchyard hangs a bell that was a gift of Queen Anne, patroness of the colonial churches.

Makemie Memorial Presbyterian Church

This church was built in 1890, the most recent of four buildings serving Presbyterian congregations in this community for three hundred years. The Snow Hill congregation was one of the first to be organized in the colonies by the Reverend Francis Makemie and goes back to 1684. The "Father of the American Presbyterian Church" visited Snow Hill early in his ministry, about the time it first became a town, since there were a considerable number of Presbyterians there from Scotland and Ulster, Ireland.

The church that honors him today is of red brick in Gothic style with two high towers and a vaulted ceiling inside with hand-hewn arches.

Furnace Town Historic Site

Where: *From Rt. 12 about 5 miles north of Snow Hill.*
A highway sign and historic marker indicate
the turn onto Old Furnace Road. Furnace
Town is to the left a short way along this road.
When: *Open April through October, 11 a.m. to 5 p.m.*
Phone: *410-632-2032*

Rising in the trees and swamp of the Pocomoke Forest, the old thirty-five-foot-high brick and stone Nassawango furnace stack is like an emblem of the past, indomitable at the heart of a vanished village.

When it was built in 1829, it was an ingenious enterprise, taking advantage of the bog iron of Nassawango Swamp, the charcoal produced from the pine of the forest, and barge transport on the nearby Pocomoke River. It was to fail only fifteen years later.

The furnace and surrounding town were originally built by the Maryland Iron Company. In 1837 the company sold seven thousand acres of forest and swamp, the furnace, a grist mill, saw mill, ironmaster's mansion house, ironworkers' houses, store barns, fixtures, and tools to Judge Thomas A. Spence. It is said that Judge Spence sank his and his wife's considerable fortunes into what seemed for a while to be a flourishing industry. The sound of the bellows reverberated through the countryside, powered by a millstream that was fed by a three-hundred-acre mill pond.

High production costs and competition in Pennsylvania and elsewhere caused its demise in 1847. Where blacksmiths, wheelwrights, cobblers, and bargemen lived and worked, and hundreds of ironworkers swarmed around the tall furnace stack, the Pocomoke Forest closed in and there remained scarcely a trace.

In 1962 the land on which Nassawango Furnace stands and where the town once thrived was given to the Worcester County Historical Society by the owners, the Foster family. The Furnace Town Foundation, Inc. was organized and continues to be supported by Worcester County civic groups, corporations, and individuals.

Archeologists and historians have studied the site. Markers identify the locations of the buildings in this briefly prosperous town and explain the working of the furnace. A small museum and a working blacksmith shop, broom-making house, smokehouse, country store, and church add interest for the visitor.

Perhaps most interesting of all is the one-mile Paul Leifer Nature Trail along Nassawango Creek and the surrounding swamp and forest land now in the stewardship of the Nature Conservancy. It begins and ends down near the old furnace and invites exploration in any season.

Furnace Town has a year-round schedule of weekend events worth checking.

The Indian Trail continues from this point to Princess Anne.

POCOMOKE CITY

I n recent years Pocomoke City has transformed its waterfront on the Pocomoke River from a neglected and weed-choked community backyard into the multi-use well-tended Cypress Park. It is the starting point for a four-mile trail with sections of floating boardwalk, exercise stations, a pedestrian bridge, fishing pier, gazebo, and canoe launch sites.

The downtown has been enlivened with brick walks and decorative street lights.

THE COSTEN HOUSE

Phone: 410-957-4364

At 204 Market Street, the Costen House is a demonstration of this small town's renewed awareness of itself. It was built in 1870 by Dr. Isaac T. Costen, Pocomoke City's first mayor. Over one hundred years later, in 1974, the town's voters were asked to decide by referendum in a local election whether it should be preserved as a historical landmark or torn down for a downtown parking lot.

It was believed to be the first time in the state that the survival of a house had been put directly to the voters on an election ballot. The house won.

With help from the Maryland Historical Trust, the local Spirit of Newtown Committee, Inc. (Newtown was this boat landing's first name) has restored the house with the typical furnishings and decor of its period. Memorial gifts have added other touches such as an adjoining Hall-Walton garden with gazebo.

It is at its best in December when decorated in Victorian style for "Christmas at Costen House."

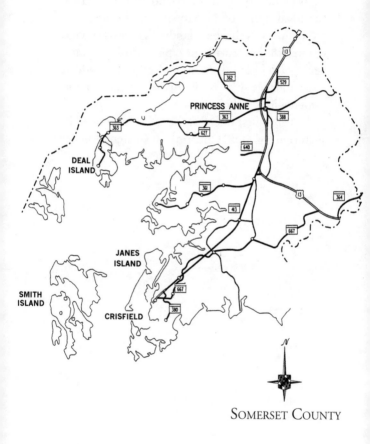

SOMERSET COUNTY

SOMERSET COUNTY

PRINCESS ANNE

*T*his Somerset County town draws visitors by its name alone. (It was named for the daughter of King George II of England.) When it became a town in 1733, it was an active port on the Manokin River, although only marsh and a narrow channel barely float a canoe today.

Princess Anne is on the National Register of Historic Places. A self-guided walking tour brochure can be had at the Tourist Information Center on U.S. 13 just south of town. It is worth a little effort to get one for full appreciation of the many historic homes and buildings along its streets.

The centerpiece of the Historic District is the Teackle Mansion.

TEACKLE MANSION

Where: At the head of Prince William Street, 2 blocks
from the Somerset County courthouse
When: Open March to mid-December, Wednesday:
1 p.m. to 3 p.m.; Saturday: 11 a.m. to 3 p.m.
Open Sunday all year: 2 p.m. to 4 p.m.
Phone: 1-800-521-9189 or 410-651-3020 or
410-651-2238
and . . . Entry fee

When Littleton Dennis Teackle built this elegant Georgian mansion in 1802, he could watch from his window his ocean-going ships on the Manokin River. In the style of the Scottish manor house he had copied, his home had a large central hall and symmetrical north and south wings. It later achieved fame as the setting for a portion of George Alfred Townsend's novel, *The Entailed Hat*, which was published in 1884 and has since had innumerable reprintings.

It is the mansion's identity with this novel that explains the top hats that are symbols of Olde Princess Anne Days, the annual October tour of historic Somerset County houses and estates that raises money for the mansion's preservation.

Much of the credit for its preservation goes to the late Maude Jeffries, a protector of historic Princess Anne, who organized its acquisition from the

owners of three sepa-
rate apartments and
persuaded donors to
part with antiques to
furnish it and painters
and plasterers to do-
nate labor and skill.
Mrs. Jeffries fought
fiercely to fend off
commercial develop-
ment that threatened

*Teackle Mansion gives special
distinction to Princess Anne, a
town as intriguing as its name.*

the mansion's surroundings, and it now looks se-
renely down Prince William Street, lined on both
sides with tree-shaded, beautifully maintained historic homes.

St. Andrews

St. Andrews was built about 1770 to serve one
of four parishes into which Somerset County was
divided. (Somerset then embraced three Lower
Shore counties.) Through the years there has been
some remodeling inside and out. The bell tower,
the gift of a parishioner, was added in the mid
nineteenth century. The lych-gate and brick wall
around the churchyard were added in 1964.

Elsewhere in this charming town, on a rise at
the north edge is . . .

Manokin Presbyterian Church

Manokin is one of five churches organized by the Reverend Francis Makemie in 1683, the first Presbyterian churches in the New World. The present church was originally built in 1765. The walls today are the original. The bell tower was added in 1888.

The Mosely Gallery, University of Maryland—Eastern Shore

Where: In the Art & Technology Building at the university campus in Princess Anne
When: Open for special exhibitions, Monday through Friday, 10 a.m. to 2 p.m.
Phone: 410-651-2200

The gallery is named in memory of Jimmie Mosely, a gifted artist and teacher who made the art department on this campus an outstanding one before his untimely death in 1974.

Its exhibitions of the work of Maryland artists and of art department faculty and students change over the year.

Eastern Shore Early Americana Museum

Where: *Near Marion Station at Hudson's Corner.*
         Reached by turning off U.S. 13 onto Rt. 413
         (the road to Crisfield). Take second left. Turn
         north at Rt. 667 and follow to its end at
         intersection where museum is visible.
When: *Open by appointment*
Phone: *410-623-8324*
and. . . : *Entry fee*

This astounding collection is the more so because of its isolated location and the ingenuity required to find it. The collector and guide has amassed an overwhelming, indiscriminate, disorganized, and absolutely fascinating conglomeration from this rural region's past piled into an old three-story chicken house, a nearby shed, a former country store, and out of doors.

Important to this museum is the presence of the collector, Lawrence W. Burgess, as guide. With his knobby walking stick, he leads the visitor down long aisles between clusters of old wooden washing machines, butter churns (including one that was operated by a goat walking on a wooden treadmill), water pumps, stoves, corn shellers and crushers, chicken brooders, toys by the bushel, early vacuum cleaners operated by a bellows-like pump, cherry pitters, sausage casers, shapers for making felt hats or shoes, and old Christmas decorations.

From the farm are rows of the harnesses and trees for hitching workhorses to wagons, calf weaners, milk cans, cream separators, sheep shearers, timber carts, early plows, and steam engines. There is the first John Deer tractor to be used on the Shore, a two-cylinder machine still workable. There are clay pigeon throwers for trap shooting, rows of mail boxes from a rural post office, two black horse-drawn hearses with glass sides, a 1901 Oldsmobile, and two antique fire engines.

Mr. Burgess describes himself as a compulsive collector. By creating his own museum about thirty years ago, he explains, he gave purpose to his collecting. He describes himself as maybe "a little crazy." If so, many an organized museum would like to have even a small portion of his "crazy" collection.

Its eventual fate is not decided, but Mr. Burgess insists that it remain unbroken. There is a point to that conviction. As it is now, it is surely one of a kind.

REHOBETH PRESBYTERIAN CHURCH

*Where: On Rt. 406 between Pocomoke City and
Crisfield, off Rt. 667*

Rehobeth is the oldest Presbyterian church in
America. It was built in 1706 by the Reverend
Francis Makemie, "Father of the American Presbyterian Church," on his own land. The Reverend Makemie had a hand in the building of four
other of the earliest churches of this denomination on the peninsula.

The interior of Rehobeth has been altered many
times, but, except for a few changes in the windows, the exterior brick walls have remained as
they were laid over two-and-a-half centuries ago.
The church is still active.

Across the road are . . .

THE RUINS OF OLD COVENTRY

Rehobeth Church, Coventry Episcopal Parish,
burned over a century ago, but its serene brick

walls and cross on the remains of its altar stand as a memorial to the church built in 1735, grand for its day, seating up to one thousand members of its congregation. Today it is silent and remote, a place for undisturbed meditation.

CRISFIELD

*T*his seafood town, calling itself the "Crab Capital of the World," has long since passed from its boom days as a bawdy port early this century to an era in which the seafood industry is barely surviving. In season ten or eleven seafood houses around the harbor still steam and pick the bay's famed blue crabs, and watermen tend rows of wooden trays in which shedding crabs will become the delicacy known as soft shells. That other delicacy—the bay oyster, once shipped out by the train carload and processed in such quantity that part of the town rests on heaps of oyster shells—is now in such short supply that the oyster cans in which they were once packed are collector's items.

Like other Eastern Shore waterfront villages, Crisfield is discovering that a vanishing way of life is its biggest attraction. Books such as William

Warner's Pulitzer Prize-winning *Beautiful Swimmers* have captured the timeless and independent way of life of the Chesapeake Bay waterman and have given Crisfield an identity from New York to Seattle.

Crisfield looks toward a future dominated by tourism and recreational boating. Far bigger than its working harbor is the state-financed, multi-million dollar Somers Cove Marina with 220 boat slips for pleasure boats, floating piers, and dockage for excursion boats taking tour groups to Smith and Tangier Islands.

The centerpiece of the expanding marina is the Tawes Visitors Center and Museum.

The citizens of Crisfield purchased this doughboy statue in 1923 as a tribute to the nine local boys who died in World War I. Memorial Day wreath-laying ceremonies ever since have honored the veterans of this and subsequent wars buried beneath the rows of headstones that surround it.

GOVERNOR J. MILLARD TAWES MUSEUM

Where: *In the Boating and Visitors Center at Somers*
              Cove Marina
When: *Open daily June through September, 10 a.m. to*
              7 p.m.; October through May, 10 a.m. to
              4 p.m.
Phone: *410-968-2501 or 1-800-782-3913*

J. Millard Tawes was a former Maryland governor (from 1958 to 1966) and Crisfield's favorite
son. His political career spanned forty-five years
during which he served as state comptroller,
Maryland's first secretary of natural resources, and
state treasurer. He died in 1979.

The new Tawes Museum provides far fancier
quarters for his memorabilia than the old and now
deserted office he used to occupy in Crisfield's
downtown. Its collection mixes the artifacts from
his long career with boat models, duck carvings,
and local crafts.

Part of its support comes from the J. Millard
Tawes Crab and Clam Bake held here every July, an
event that draws about thirty-five hundred persons
and is one of the state's biggest informal gatherings
of state and local politicians. For candidates in com-
ing elections, it is an event not to be overlooked.

WARD BROTHERS HOMEPLACE

Where: *In Crisfield on Sackertown Road*
When: *Open daily May through mid-October, 10 a.m.*
to 3 p.m.
Phone: *410-968-2501*

Lem and Steve Ward, the Crisfield brothers who "never went anywhere" but are remembered with affection and respect throughout the wide world of wildfowl carving, worked all their lives in a backyard shop next to the barbershop in which they earned their livelihoods.

The workshop has been recreated in the multi-million dollar Ward Museum of Wildfowl Art in Salisbury and contains a collection of the brothers' own favorite pieces.

A group of friends and admirers called Ward Brothers Homeplace, Inc., financially assisted by the Maryland Historical Trust and led by Jack Schroeder, a professional wildlife artist who settled in Crisfield, has restored the original workshop on Sackertown Road to be open to visitors. It contains the brothers' carving tools and a few of their unfinished birds, as if they had just stepped out. It is managed by the Tawes Museum at Somers Cove.

SMITH ISLAND

*C*risfield is the jumping-off place for a favorite Eastern Shore adventure—a boat trip to Smith Island thirteen miles out between Tangier Sound and Chesapeake Bay.

Long indifferent to tourism, the islanders have recently joined with Somerset County and Maryland agencies in creating a brochure identifying points of interest for self-guided walking tours of its three villages: Ewell, Rhodes Point, and Tylerton. Part of the island's attraction is what you won't find there—no sidewalks, beaches, convenience stores, boat rentals, movie theaters, liquor stores, bars, fast food chains, boutiques, or amusement parks. What it does have is watermen going about their business of oystering, crabbing, or watching over their family-sized soft crab shedding operations.

The simple streets of Ewell on Smith Island have the allure of timelessness and the mystique of islands.

Among the points of interest are . . .

Middleton House

Middleton House in Ewell is an interpretive center and headquarters for the Martin National Wildlife Refuge for the United States Department of the Interior's Fish and Wildlife Service, and . . .

The Chesapeake Bay Foundation's Environmental and Education Center

This center on Tylerton educates both students and adults with three-day seminar programs on bay and marsh ecology.

Visitors can get to the island by . . .

The Captain Jasons I & II

Operated by Captains Terry and Larry Laird
410-425-5931 or 410-425-4471

These boats operate year-round carrying mail, supplies, and passengers to the island. They depart from Crisfield's City Dock at the end of Rt. 413. Departure from Crisfield is 12:30 p.m. and 5 p.m. (4:30 p.m. in winter). Departure from Smith Island for the return trip is 7:30 a.m. and 4 p.m. (3:30 p.m. in winter). There are seasonal weekend departures from Ewell at 7:30 p.m. Friday and Sunday and from Crisfield at 8:30 p.m. Friday and Sunday.

ISLAND BELLE II AND *ISLAND PRINCESS*

Operated by Captain Otis Ray Tyler
410-968-3206

These boats operate in season from Crisfield's City Dock, departing at 12:30 p.m., offering an optional family-style luncheon at Harbor Side Restaurant in Ewell, and returning at 4 p.m.

THE *CAPTAIN TYLER II*

Operated by Captain Tyler II
Memorial Day through October daily
410-425-2771

Captain Tyler offers package cruises in a 150-passenger paddlewheeler departing from Somers Cove in Crisfield at 12:30 p.m. and returning at 5 p.m. The package includes a family-style seafood dinner at Captain Tyler's Bayside Inn and a bus tour of the island.

ALSO OF NOTE

FAIRMOUNT ACADEMY

Where: At Upper Fairmount on Rt. 361 off of Rt. 413
        (the road toward Crisfield)
When: Open by appointment
Phone: 410-651-0351

The rural, two-story, early nineteenth-century schoolhouse closed here in 1969 but survives as a community symbol and museum through the efforts of the Fairmount Academy Historical Association.

An annual "1800s Festival" in May combines entertainment, nostalgia, a demonstration class from academy days, and a countywide spelling bee for the students of today.

Proceeds go to the maintenance of the old schoolhouse in Academy Grove.

JOSHUA THOMAS CHURCH ON DEAL ISLAND

Where: On Rt. 363 east of U.S. 13

In the marshy lowlands of the Lower Shore along the Chesapeake Bay, white frame churches with attached steeples seem to crop up every few miles, and they are all Methodist. On Smith Island and nearby Tangier Island, across the Virginia line, there are only Methodist churches.

The reason for this is Joshua Thomas, the "Parson of the Islands," an evangelist born in 1776 on Potato Neck in Somerset County. He preached his first sermon in nearby Hopewell. Sailing from village to village and island to island in his fAmed log canoe called "The Methodist," he preached at small isolated churches and big camp meetings.

In 1814 when British ships were on their way up Chesapeake Bay to attack Baltimore, he preached to the troops on Tangier Island. He dwelt with fervor on the commandment "Thou shalt not kill" and predicted British defeat.

When his prediction was true and the British sailed back down the bay to Tangier, both the troops and the populace regarded him as prophet and hero. Joshua Thomas Day is still observed every year in churches such as this one on Deal Island, where he is buried.

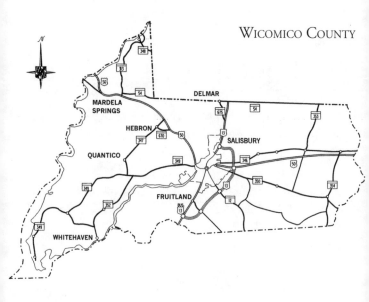

WICOMICO COUNTY

DELMAR

MARDELA
SPRINGS

HEBRON

SALISBURY

QUANTICO

FRUITLAND

WHITEHAVEN

WICOMICO COUNTY

SALISBURY

*S*alisbury, strung out in seemingly form-less fashion east to west along U.S. 50 and north to south along U.S. 13, is the commercial hub of the Lower Shore, and it looks it. A visitor who lingers for a closer look will discover off the highways, behind the auto dealerships, fast food restaurants, motels, and malls surprisingly exten-sive up-scale residential areas, a community-minded populace, and one of the Eastern Shore's most notable museums—the Ward Museum of Wildfowl Art.

WARD MUSEUM OF WILDFOWL ART

Where: At 909 South Schumaker Drive
  (Turn south off U.S. 50 at Beaglin Park Drive)
When: Open Monday through Saturday, 10 a.m. to
  5 p.m.; Sunday, noon to 5 p.m.
Phone: 410-742-4988
and . . . Entry fee

The collection of wildfowl carving at the museum in Salisbury is the best and most complete

An eye-catching snowy owl is part of the world-class collection of wildfowl carvings on display at the Ward Museum in Salisbury.

display anywhere of an art form that has developed before one's very eyes over the last twenty-five years.

The museum is named for Lem and Steve Ward, the Crisfield brothers who transformed the carving of utilitarian hunting decoys into art objects sought by galleries and collectors. The $5 million structure on Schumaker Mill Pond is in stark contrast to the tiny outbuilding in a Crisfield backyard where the brothers once carved decoys for eighteen dollars a dozen, nailed them to the inside of oyster barrels, and shipped them to customers.

A re-creation of the workshop is one of the museum displays, as is the brothers' personal collection of seventy-two favorite pieces.

In the various galleries, working decoys are displayed in marshy settings with recorded sound effects. The "Best in the World" decoys and decorative carvings from the annual World Championship Carving Competitions have been added to the collection since 1971.

The museum was the project of the Ward Foundation, organized in 1968 by a group of Salisbury businessmen, decoy collectors, and carvers. From a modest start it has grown to a membership of ten thousand extending across the nation and into Canada. It publishes two monthly newsletters and a glossy quarterly called *Wildfowl Art.*

The museum was first housed in the wing of a building on the campus of Salisbury State University, quarters that soon became too crowded for the Foundation's world-class collection. The new museum was years in the planning and required a major grant from the state.

Shortly before his death at the age of eighty-three, Lem Ward, still living in his modest home in Crisfield, estimated that he and his brother had probably carved about twenty-five thousand decoys since 1918. "They're all over the world today," he said. "I never went anywhere. I never had any money, and I never missed it. I love the people

around here and they love me. What more can
you have?"

THE SALISBURY ZOO

Where: *Between North Park and South Park Drive,*
east of U.S. 13 and south of U.S. 50
When: *Between Memorial Day and Labor Day open*
daily, 8:30 a.m. to 7:30 p.m. Otherwise,
8:30 a.m. to 4:30 p.m.
Phone: *410-548-3188*

The distinction of Salisbury's widely hailed zoo
is its limitation. It is devoted exclusively to wildlife from the two American continents, and it does
not have the distraction of concessions selling soft
drinks and snacks.

Here there are no lonely elephants or giraffes
or pacing tigers in cages. "Small children like
small animals," in the opinion of one of this
zoo's able and imaginative directors. They can
discover the Patagonian cavy, for instance, a ro-
dent that looks like a long-legged rabbit with a
kangaroo's face, or the miniature Goeldi mon-
keys from the Amazon.

The biggest animals are the bison that roam in a
large grassy fenced-in area shaded by loblolly pine
and bounded on one side by an elevated boardwalk

from which they, and the animals and birds that share their space, can be watched.

The most dramatic of the animals are the two jaguars lounging in a roomy enclosure; the most appealing, the spectacled bears belonging to a rare species in the remote highlands of Bolivia, Columbia, Equador, and Peru.

Appropriate to the zoo's location between the ocean and the bay is its collection of waterfowl, one of the most complete to be found any-

The special appeal of the Salisbury Zoo is the limitation of its collection of wildlife to the two American continents only.

where. Ducks, geese, herons swim and wade freely on an arm of the Wicomico River and can be watched and identified from a platform over the water. A short drive eastward farther along this river will bring the visitor to the Ward Museum of Wildfowl Art, where the nation's best carvers have re-created many of the zoo waterfowl's counterparts in wood.

The zoo and surrounding park attract bus loads of school children and family picnics. It is a good experience.

THE OBELISK IN SALISBURY'S DOWNTOWN PLAZA

Salisbury's seven-sided, thirty-foot-high geometric aluminum obelisk was dedicated in 1970

Salisbury's Obelisk is a memorial to past leadership and a symbol of present-day progress.

as a memorial to Fred P. Adkins, a highly respected community and business leader. At the same time, it was intended to be a symbol of the progressive spirit of the town. It was a joint project of the Fred P. Adkins Memorial Committee and the Wicomico Council of the Arts.

The project's initiators commissioned Alfredo Halegua, a native of Uruguay with a studio in Silver Spring, to design the sculpture. About one hundred Salisbury people contributed to the $30,000 cost, with a lion's share given by Wye Institute, a foundation-type organization conceived and supported by Arthur A. Houghton Jr., owner of the Shore's Wye Plantation and chairman of the board of Steuben Glass.

The initial obelisk, done in concrete, was rejected because of surface imperfections and was redone in something called "detacouple," a metallic hybrid that has sanded aluminum on the exterior and steel in the interior. Its finish and geometric planes reflect in different ways from different angles.

Today the Salisbury sculpture is listed as one of twenty-nine major works by Mr. Halegua in public places and museum collections, including the National Gallery of Art in Washington and the Baltimore Museum of Art.

SALISBURY ART INSTITUTE AND GALLERY, INC.

Where: *In Salisbury's Downtown Plaza*
When: *Open Monday through Saturday, noon to*
       4 p.m.
Phone: *410-546-4748*

The arts, so belittled in the political scheme of things in the 1980s, have become, at last, the answer to the survival and future of Salisbury's Downtown Plaza.

The Salisbury Art Institute and Gallery, Inc., a convergence of several organizations scattered over many locations, opened its newest and most extensive quarters yet in December 1995 in the vacant Woolworth building in the heart of the Plaza.

The Plaza, a beautifully landscaped pedestrian mall lined with distinctive Victorian structures, had become a center of failing retail establishments. Its life was being drained by malls, medical centers, motor vehicles, postal and other government services on the outer fringes of town.

Paralleling the move of the community arts center, four private art gallery and craft stores have occupied vacant space on the Plaza, coordinated their activities with the Art Institute and Gallery and their openings with each other, and led the city fathers to designate the old downtown as the city's new and official Arts District.

The Art Institute and Gallery features excellent one-artist and juried shows. The private galleries will surprise and delight any visitor with the originaįity and sophistication of their offerings.

A stroll through Salisbury's Downtown will show that the visual arts have achieved what no previous plan or study had considered. They have brought new life and vitality where past retail and commercial ventures had failed.

POPLAR HILL MANSION AND NEWTOWN

Where: At 117 Elizabeth Street
When: Open Sunday, 1 p.m. to 4 p.m.
Phone: 410-749-1776
and . . . Entry fee

Salisbury's Newtown is actually its old town. It is the name of the Historic District, the streets along which rambling Victorian homes were built after two big Salisbury fires in 1860 and 1886 destroyed most of the early town. Newtown was rapidly becoming the shabby part of town when, in the early 1970s, the spacious old houses began to attract young people with the energy and imagination to fix them up and turn this into the most colorful section of Salisbury. The focal point of the district's restoration was Poplar Hill Mansion.

Poplar Hill Mansion survived two big Salisbury fires and gives to the Victorian Newtown a touch of eighteenth-century elegance.

Poplar Hill is not Victorian. It is a survivor of the fires, a rare holdover from the eighteenth century and believed to be the oldest building in Salisbury. It is a symmetrical white frame house of elegant simplicity, described as country Georgian style. The entrance is enhanced by a fan-shaped window over the front door and a Palladian-type window directly above on the second story. The wide entrance hall is made light and inviting by another Palladian window in the back, rising from the landing of the wide stairway.

Its elegance comes not from splendor, but from the beauty of its woodwork—the cornices and dentil molding, the archway in the entrance hall, the chair railings, stairway, fluted pilasters, and mantels.

The mansion is now owned and maintained by the City of Salisbury, which appoints members to the board of Friends of Poplar Hill Mansion, Inc. to run it. It is a place for parties, wedding receptions, musicales and the like, made all the more memorable by a touch of class. It is probably enjoyed by more people today than at any time in its past.

CHIPMAN CULTURAL CENTER

*Where: At the corner of Broad and Ellen Streets, close
          to the juncture of U.S. 13 and U.S. 50*
When: Open by appointment
Phone: 410-860-9290

On a rise overlooking the steady traffic where the Shore's two major highways cross in Salisbury, a plain, white frame, two-story structure offers little clue to the passersby of its significance.

This is the original A.M.E. Church, the oldest black church on the Eastern Shore and one of the oldest in the country still standing. The land on which it stands was simply an open field on a hill when it was purchased from the white owner in

1837 by three freedmen. For many years before that, black people had gathered in this field for worship services with itinerant MethodIST PREACH-ERS, THe only ones responding to their call.

A portion of the present structure was built in 1838 and was part of the Philadelphia conference of the African Methodist Church. All other black churches in Salisbury today have their roots in the old church on the hill.

Some years ago the late Charles P. Chipman, a remarkable Salisbury educator, and his wife, Jeanette Pinkett Chipman, bought the old building from the Peninsula General Conference. "I was always happy to come to this church," he once said, "and I didn't want to see it destroyed."

Dr. Chipman had come to Salisbury in 1915 as principal of the then Colored Industrial High School, later to become the all-black Salisbury High School. He held that position for forty-six years and with his gentle leadership earned the respect of all segments of the community.

Before his death in 1987, Dr. Chipman gave the deed to the old church to the Chipman Foundation along with the hope that it would be restored as a meeting place and museum of black history and culture.

That hope is now being fulfilled. With the co-operation of Salisbury's Newtown Association, a matching grant from the Maryland General Assembly, and a loan from the Maryland Historical

Trust, the structure has a new roof and other structural improvements and beautifully refinished floors and pews inside.

A grand opening on May 1, 1994, introduced it to the community as a place for meetings, gospel sings, weddings, and catered functions.

It has still to reach its potential for use and community awareness, but is a great step forward toward integrating Salisbury's heritage as well as its public life.

SALISBURY STATE UNIVERSITY GALLERIES

ATRIUM GALLERY

Where: *Guerrieri University Center*
When: *Open Monday through Friday, 11 a.m. to*
4 p.m.; Saturday and Sunday, noon to 4 p.m.
Phone: *410-543-6271*

FULTON HALL GALLERY

When: *Open Tuesday through Thursday, 10 a.m. to*
5 P.M.; FRIDAY, 10 A.M. TO 8 P.M.; SATURDAY and
Sunday, noon to 4 p.m.
Phone: *410-543-6270*

Both galleries offer first-class shows of works by outstanding artists living on the Shore and on loan from elsewhere.

ROCKAWALKIN SCHOOL

Where: *On Pemberton Drive on the grounds of Pemberton School*

When: *Open by request by calling 410-742-8805, or by obtaining key in Pemberton School office.*

This one-room school was built for the rural Wicomico County community of Rockawalkin about 1872 and was attended by the children of that area until 1939. It contains mementos of the school's past and pictures of former classes.

It was moved to its present site in 1973 by a group of former students who raised the money and got official support. It has now been taken over by the Wicomico Historical Society, Inc.

DELMARVA RESEARCH CENTER FOR HISTORY AND CULTURE

Where: *At Power and Wayne Streets in Salisbury State University's Power Professional Building*

When: *Open September through May, Monday through Friday: 9 a.m. to 4 p.m. Closed on school holidays. Check summer hours*
Phone: *410-543-6312*

For the serious researcher, the center offers a growing archive of historical documents related to the region. It also has on microfilm some of the oldest records in the nation from the courthouse in Eastville on the Virginia Eastern Shore and from the Hall of Records in Annapolis. There are surveyor records going back to the nineteenth century that are still used in official title searches.

The center has acquired Hodson Old Home Prize essays from Eastern Shore high schools, and documents, maps, books, and journals from private donors. It is collecting taped interviews for an oral history section.

NUTTER'S ELECTION HOUSE

Where: *At South Division Street in Fruitland on the grounds of the town water plant*
When: *Visits by appointment only. Write Wicomico Historical Society, P.O. Box 212, Salisbury, Maryland 21801*

The Wicomico County Historical Society is developing an unusual museum in this sixty-year-old, onetime polling place. It will house memorabilia—campaign buttons, handbills, posters, and the like—from nineteenth- and twentieth-century local, state, and federal elections. The collection includes photographs of candidates, registration lists, and sample ballots.

Maryland Lady Cruises

Where: From the Port of Salisbury just south of U.S. 50
When: By reservation
Phone: 410-543-2466

A replica of the old sidewheel riverboat takes passengers on sightseeing, lunch, and dinner cruises down the Wicomico River, one of the most underrated of the Shore's scenic rivers. The river is narrow and winding, giving passengers close-up views that range from elegant contemporary homes on the outskirts of Salisbury to wild expanses of marshland.

Pemberton Historical Park

Where: About 2 miles southwest of Salisbury. From
U.S. 50, turn west onto Rt. 349. Turn left onto
Pemberton Drive. Continue about 2 miles to
entrance gate on the left.

When: *Park open daily, 8 a.m. to sunset; house open*
           May through October, Sunday: 2 p.m. to 4 p.m.
Phone: *410-749-0124 or 410-548-4900*

Pemberton Historical Park includes the 1741 Pemberton Hall house museum, the Wicomico Historical Society museum, a picnic area, and nature trails.

The restoration of Pemberton Hall took longer to achieve than its original construction in 1741. It is a gem of a heritage house. As it was slowly

Pemberton Hall, one of the earliest gambrel roofed houses in Maryland, is part of a 207-acre park that also includes a Heritage Center, nature walks, and marsh observation platforms.

brought to new life by tenacious organizers of Pemberton Hall Foundation, it became the centerpiece of a complex that includes a Heritage Center for the Wicomico County Historical Society, Inc. and a Wicomico County park and nature walk with explanatory markers and platforms for observing marsh life. Leading from the walk are over four miles of walking trails.

The house was originally built by Colonel Isaac Handy, a sea captain, planter, and early developer of Salisbury town. It is said to be one of the earliest gambrel roofed houses in Maryland. Its bricks are laid in Flemish bond, and its new roof is of cedar shingles.

The county has acquired 207 acres around it so that it stands in the midst of open fields, woodland, and marsh that have not changed substantially in 250 years.

Two new structures have been patterned after the tobacco barns of the colonial period with such meticulous care that they could be surviving outbuildings of the early plantation. One houses restrooms and equipment of the recreation and parks department, and the other is the headquarters, museum, and gift shop of the historical society.

ALSO OF NOTE

OLD GREEN HILL NEAR WHITEHAVEN

Where: Twelve miles west of Salisbury on Rt. 352

Old Green Hill Church has looked out on the Wicomico River from its tree-shaded knoll since 1733. When it was built, Whitehaven, a short distance down the river, was a thriving port of entry for the lower Eastern Shore. The church served a wide-ranging Episcopal parish extending all the way into what is now southern Delaware.

Today it appears lonely but is not quite forsaken; it is opened for an annual service in August.

Inside, the floors of the sanctuary and nave are of brick. There are high family pews with seats on three sides and a door at the entrance.

Its date of construction is proclaimed in black brick under the east gable.

WHITEHAVEN HERITAGE ASSOCIATION

Where: *2764 Whitehaven Road in Whitehaven*
When: *Open by request*
Phone: *410-873-2939 or 410-548-4914*

Whitehaven has had past lives as a colonial port, shipbuilding center, steamboat port, and even, in the 1920s, rum runners' landing. Today, far off the beaten track of commerce and tourism, it is one of the Shore's most delightful waterfront villages. Most of its residents have working lives elsewhere—some as far away as Washington—but have created here a very special sense of place and community.

In a well-maintained, late nineteenth-century schoolhouse, the heritage association keeps a collection of Whitehaven documents and art and holds community events.

At the waterfront, the historic Whitehaven Ferry has operated here since 1690. It is now a steel vessel holding two or three cars, guided by cable. It carries commuters across the Wicomico River between Wicomico and Somerset Counties. It is a crossing that also attracts bicycle clubs and sightseers who have detached themselves from the usual routes.

CHESAPEAKE FIRE MUSEUM

Where: *In Hebron on the west side of Rt. 670*
When: *Open Monday through Friday, 9 a.m. to 5 p.m.; or by appointment*
Phone: *410-546-3117*

The creators of this museum make clear that it is not intended to be a diversion but a learning experience, with special appeal to fellow firemen. It surprises with its extensiveness—eleven thousand square feet of exhibit space—and for the display of hand-drawn, horse-drawn, and engine-powered equipment and artifacts of the fire fighter.

It is the project of a public non-profit foundation and is known to the National Organization of Fire Museums for its expert restorations. It has traded off restoration work for some of the artifacts in its collection.

The thrust of this museum, says Charles Black, an initiator and spokesman, is the commitment of the volunteer fireman and community service as a way of life.

This museum does not advertise itself nor seek to be identified as a tourist attraction, but nonetheless has about two thousand visitors a year.

ADKINS MUSEUM AND HISTORICAL COMPLEX

Where: *On Main and Brattan Streets in Mardela*
When: *Open by request*
Phone: *410-749-4871*

J. Howard and Louise H. Adkins have amassed a private collection that has grown to museum proportions. It includes not only artifacts, books, and documents, but buildings. Their complex includes a village general store, a nineteenth-century one-room school, a small two-story farmhouse dated about 1720, a long white frame one-time livery stable, and a one-time Wicomico County election house.

The complex has given impetus to a West Side Historical Society devoted to rural Wicomico County, less traveled than the more familiar Salisbury area.

Though the restored buildings are impressive, the heart of their collection is books. The early school readers, spellers, and geographies; collected sermons; annual almanacs; and travel guides invite hours of browsing.

MASON DIXON MARKERS

Where: On Rt. 54, about midway between Delmar and Mardela

Two simple stones in a shelter on this lonely rural road have a significance in Maryland and Delaware history beyond their appearance. They are the cornerstones for the east-west and north-south boundary of Delaware in settlement of a long-running boundary dispute between the families of William Penn and Lord Baltimore. Maryland was the loser.

The smaller and more weathered marker was placed by a team of surveyors in 1760 following an initial survey in 1750. The trouble was, according to historians, that the east-west line was supposed to have started from Cape Henlopen,

On a lonely rural road, these cornerstones for the boundary between Delaware and Maryland have an importance in the history of both states that has been all but forgotten.

but because of dubious geographical references on the official map used by the initial surveyors, it was started fifteen miles to the south at what is actually Fenwick.

The big stone in the shelter is the double crownstone placed there in 1768 after Charles Mason and Jeremiah Dixon were brought to this country by the two proprietors to lead the survey. They accepted the midpoint that had been established eight years earlier and proceeded to run the tangent line north. Thus a chunk of land about fifteen miles long and thirty-three miles wide, including what is now Delaware's beach resort area, became the property of the Penns instead of Lord Baltimore.

The third stone in the shelter has no explanation, nor can one be found.

MID SHORE

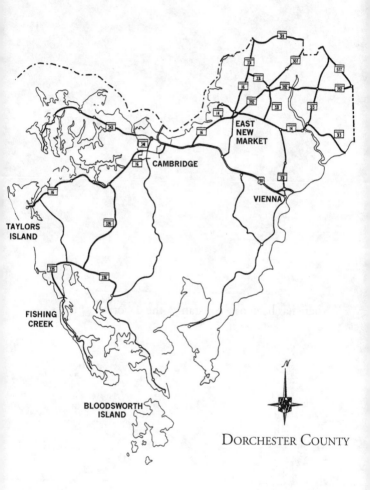

TAYLORS
ISLAND

CAMBRIDGE

EAST
NEW
MARKET

VIENNA

FISHING
CREEK

BLOODSWORTH
ISLAND

N

DORCHESTER COUNTY

DORCHESTER COUNTY

This Mid Shore county and its county seat of Cambridge have a character of their own that resists description with the generalities that apply to either the Upper or the Lower Shore. Theirs has been a history of ups and downs, political, social, and economic. But there has been one constant—the devotion of the inhabitants to fishing, hunting, and trapping for sport and for livelihood. The spacious Victorian and Edwardian homes along Cambridge's High Street reflect old family money once made in farming, canning, and seafood packing. The houses of five former Maryland governors are in Cambridge. But the real character of the region is still shaped by the vast expanses of marsh that make up most of its land area, and the rivers, bays, creeks, coves, and mosquito ditches that cut into it.

A drive into the depths of Dorchester's marshland east of Cambridge and down toward Blackwater Wildlife Refuge, Taylors Island, or Honga
is worth the distance and time just for the feel of
its emptiness and awareness of the wealth of natural life in the wetlands.

WALKING AND DRIVING TOUR INFORMATION

*Where: In Cambridge: Dorchester County Tourism
        Office, 501 Court Lane; or the Visitor's Center,
        203 Sunburst Highway (U.S. 50)*
Phone: 1-800-522-TOUR; 410-228-1000

Brochures for a forty-five-minute walking
tour of Cambridge's historic district and a more
extensive two-hour tour, walking tours of the
National Historic District in East New Market
and the old port town of Vienna, and a driving
tour of Dorchester County are available at the
Dorchester County Tourism Office or the
Visitor's Center.

CAMBRIDGE

The Sculpture of the Grand National Waterfowl Hunt

As a motorist crosses the Choptank into Dorchester County, he is welcomed by a sixteen-foot-high concrete monolith on which sixteen bronze life-size geese are grouped in a landing pattern. They are the work of George Northup, a wildlife artist of Jackson Hole, Wyoming. It was the project of participants in the county's annual Grand National Waterfowl Hunt, an event attracting celebrities from across the nation as well as local outdoorsmen.

To help pay for the $125,000 work, there was one duplicate casting of each of the sixteen geese, each sold to an individual or company. The sculpture was dedicated on December 18, 1989. (The sculpture was removed temporarily to accommodate construction of a visitors center. It will be returned when the building is completed.)

DORCHESTER COUNTY HISTORICAL SOCIETY COMPLEX

Where: *On Maryland Avenue three blocks east of U.S. 50 near the east end of Choptank River bridge.*
When: *Open Thursday through Saturday, 10 a.m. to 4 p.m.*
Phone: *410-228-7953*
and . . . Entry fee

There are two separate and quite different museums on the Historical Society grounds in Cambridge. One is the Meredith House, a brick Georgian townhouse furnished as it might have been by its prosperous early owners. The other, the Neild Museum, recaptures the way of life of the local watermen and farmers through the years. A smaller structure, the Goldsborough Stable, dates from about 1790 and houses exhibits related to nineteenth-century transportation.

MEREDITH HOUSE

Built on land originally occupied by a nation of Indians called the Ababcos, the Meredith House has passed through many ownerships from the Revolutionary War to 1959, when it was bought by the Dorchester County Historical Society.

It is of brick laid in Flemish bond with balanced design and carved wooden cornices reflecting the influence of English architecture in vogue at the time it was built. Its rooms contain a delightful collection of antique dolls and the memorabilia related to six Maryland governors who came from Dorchester County in an era when the Eastern Shore's landed gentry had a powerful voice in state government.

From the gracious Meredith House, the visitor can walk across the lawn to a more rustic sample of Dorchester's heritage.

NEILD MUSEUM

Here in a quiet, architecturally appropriate, and little-publicized museum are exhibits dedicated to the farmers, watermen, and trappers who have given the county its distinctive character. Because of the volunteer talent and labor that went into it, from fill dirt

Dorchester County's Neild Museum, preserving the artifacts of farm, home, and seafood harvest, is part of a complex that also includes a Georgian townhouse, historic stable, and herb garden.

to construction and landscaping, it reflects Dorchester County community life today as much as the past it preserves.

Along with the old wooden tools of farm and home are photographs belonging to Annie Oakley, the Wild West show markswoman who once lived in Cambridge. There are also the remarkable collections of Indian arrowheads, stone tools, and pottery shards discovered in the county by its two premier collectors, the late Judge William B. Yates II and William T. Keene.

SAILWINDS PARK

Where: *Beside the Dorchester General Hospital, at Cambridge's former industrial port site*
Phone: *410-228-SAIL*

Where Cambridge once hoped to develop a thriving industrial port, local and state governments are now turning the Choptank River waterfront into a park with an innovative playground, farmers' market, boat rentals, festival grounds, and visitors' center. Already the old port building has been converted into an exhibition and concert hall. Enthusiastic civic leaders promise lots more to come. For anyone unfamiliar with Cambridge and what it has to offer, even a drive through will give a sense of discovery.

THE STACK AT CAMBRIDGE'S LONG WHARF

At Long Wharf on the Choptank River at the foot of Cambridge's historic High Street, a black and white ship's stack might attract only a casual glance, if the visitor did not pause to read the bronze plaque beside it. It was erected "In memory of Franklin Delano Roosevelt, a great American who visited Cambridge October 26, 1935, to participate in the dedication of the Governor Emerson C. Harrington bridge. The stack is from the *U.S.S. Potomac* which carried the president ... on numerous historic occasions. It enclosed the elevator which meant so much to his comfort."

The bridge that President Roosevelt traveled up the Choptank to help dedicate was replaced in the spring of 1988 by a new one. The old bridge,

The black and white ship's stack at Cambridge's Long Wharf is from the U.S.S. Potomac and once enclosed the elevator used by President Franklin Delano Roosevelt.

taken over by the state Department of Natural Resources, is now a popular fishing pier.

"THE PATIENT FISHER"

To celebrate the completion of the new Choptank River Bridge, the Dorchester Arts Council planned to erect the county's first public

sculpture at the bridge's entrance into the county. The center commissioned the work from a Maryland wildlife artist, John Neal Mullican of Bowie, and set out to raise about $35,000 for a life-size bronze of the great blue heron.

By the time of its completion, its location had been changed to its present city park site next to Long Wharf; the site by the bridge was given to still another sculpture. "The Patient Fisher," a name derived from an Indian word for the elegant heron, was

"The Patient Fisher," a life-size bronze heron at Long Wharf, was a gift to the community by the Dorchester Arts Council.

unveiled on June 16, 1989, and dedicated to Blackwater National Wildlife Refuge, the people of Dorchester, and their common respect for the county's wetlands and wildlife.

THE NATHAN OF DORCHESTER

Where: At Long Wharf at the foot of High Street
When: For information, call 410-228-7141

The forty-five-foot wooden skipjack now available for inspection and charter is special not only for what it is, but for how it came to be. This traditional oystering boat of the Chesapeake is the first to be built in many years and was conceived and constructed by local volunteers, most of whom had never done anything like it before.

The project was sponsored by a specially organized Skipjack Committee and directed by two skilled boat builders. It took two and one-half years to complete. The money for it came from donations and a trust fund established by the late Milford Nathan, for whom it is named.

It is one of several projects underway here to bring new life and vitality to Cambridge's waterfronts.

DORCHESTER ARTS CENTER

Where: *At 120 High Street*
When: *Open Monday through Friday, 10 a.m. to*
        2 p.m.; Saturday, 11 a.m. to 3 p.m.
Phone : 410-228-7782

In one of the big old houses along the brick street of Cambridge's Historic District, the Arts Center has three galleries in which exhibitions of local paintings, sculpture, and crafts change monthly.

On the fourth Sunday of September, the center has its annual Dorchester Showcase, a juried show for which High Street is lined with about one hundred booths. Art is combined with good food and entertainment.

RICHARDSON MUSEUM

Where: *At 401 High Street, corner of High and Locust*
When: *Open mid-April through October; Wednesday,*
        Saturday, Sunday; 1 p.m. to 4 p.m. or by
        appointment
Phone: *1-800-522-TOUR*

This newly opened museum in a former bank building in the heart of Cambridge's downtown is named for James B. Richardson, master shipwright of the Chesapeake, and dedicated to the wooden boat builders of Dorchester County. Its exhibits are selective, featuring superb models of boats built by local craftsmen and the special tools of the boatbuilder.

The Hall of Fame offers exhibits relating to the remarkable number of Dorchester Countians active in national power-boat racing.

There is a special "Mr. Jim" room in which the visitor can come to know the long heritage continued and passed on by Jim Richardson. During his boatbuilding years, Mr. Jim was sought out at his boatyard on LeCompte Bay, a small tidal inlet off the lower Choptank River, by admirers from everywhere. The first Richardsons came to this country and opened a boatyard near what is now Federal Hill in Baltimore sometime in the early 1600s. They eventually moved to the Eastern Shore for better access to timber near the water. When Mr. Jim started his boatyard, his father warned that it would be unprofitable, an assessment that was correct; but the boatyard rewarded him at any rate with honors, recognition, and a working life doing something he loved.

Mr. Jim was master of a dying art of building, not from detailed blue prints, but from a carved wooden model. He informed the boat building scenes in James Michener's *Chesapeake,* built the replica of the *Dove* now sailing out of historic St. Marys City, and gave of himself to a stream of visitors, young and old, who sought to learn his craft and be in his company.

His shipyard on LeCompte Bay is now idle, but a nephew has a busy shipyard in Cambridge called Generation III.

The museum bearing his name had support from the Maryland Historical Trust.

BRANNOCK MARITIME MUSEUM

Where: At 210 Talbot Avenue
When: Open Friday and Saturday, 10 a.m. to 4 p.m.;
Sunday, 1 p.m. to 4 p.m.; or by appointment
Phone: 410-228-6938
and . . . Entry fee

Earl and Shirley Brannock's private museum is polished in every way. Its floors and exhibits gleam like the wooden fittings of a tall ship at a Bicentennial celebration. And the ship models, photographs of ships' captains, old prints, documents, and artifacts on display make it a beautifully organized storehouse of discoveries for casual visitors or scholars—or for the many schoolchildren who are brought here.

Mr. Brannock is a product of Cambridge's maritime heritage, working the water in his boyhood summers under his uncle, Captain Amos Creighton, skipper of the governor's yachts, the *Governor McLean* and later the *Dupont*. He was

The Brannock Maritime Museum is a private one that preserves, with documents, old prints, and artifacts, the maritime heritage of both the Brannock family and Cambridge.

also head of what was then known as the Oyster Navy, a fleet of about forty boats enforcing the regulations of the Tidewater Fisheries during a period extending into the early 1940s. This was a time when Maryland and Virginia watermen were engaged in a conflict over fishing rights so violent it is still known as the Oyster Wars.

Memorabilia from Captain Creighton's adventures on the Chesapeake and artifacts he had inherited from his father and grandfathers relating to lifetimes in coastal shipping and other water-related ventures begin the exhibition. Mr. Brannock has expanded his collection into this nation's naval and maritime history, including the Revolutionary War, Civil War, and both World Wars.

Two local heroes of more peaceable days are featured in this museum. One is Captain Orville Parks, who captained the skipjack *Rosie Parks* to so many victories in the annual skipjack races at Deal Island and Sandy Point that it is now a floating exhibit at the Chesapeake Bay Maritime Museum at St. Michaels. The other is James B. Richardson, known far and wide as the master shipwright of the Chesapeake and named "Admiral of the Chesapeake" by Governor Harry Hughes in 1979.

To Earl Brannock's devotion to Chesapeake lore is added Shirley Brannock's talent as a watercolorist of bay-related subjects.

Still another asset worth noting is the attachment of bed-and-breakfast quarters to their backyard museum.

Harriet Tubman Sites

Harriet Tubman, one of the most remarkable of Eastern Shore heroines, was born into slavery in Dorchester County in 1820. She escaped in 1849 at the age of twenty-nine, but she returned again and again to lead over three hundred slaves to freedom through the Underground Railroad. She was known then and is remembered now as the "Moses of Her People."

During the Civil War, she served the Union Army as nurse, scout, and spy.

While there is no formal monument or shrine in the county of her birth, her memory is alive in the activities of the Harriet Tubman Coalition, an organization that sponsors tours and events in her honor.

Only this lonely historic marker amid fields of soybeans and corn identifies the birthplace of Harriet Tubman, the remarkable woman known as the "Moses of her People."

THE UNDERGROUND RAILROAD:
HARRIET TUBMAN MUSEUM AND GIFT SHOP
HEADQUARTERS, HARRIET TUBMAN
COALITION

Where: At 424 Race Street
Phone: 410-228-0401

Not actually a museum, this is a center for the organization of Tubman-related activities. From here, the coalition organizes tours that include the birthplace of Harriet Tubman, now identified only by a lonely historic marker on Green Briar Road amid a wide expanse of corn and soybean fields and empty landscape.

There is also the small wood-frame Bazel Church on Bestpitch Ferry Road nearby, which she attended and where services are held the third Sunday in June each year in her honor.

Coalition tours are organized as well for local people to Auburn, New York, where Harriet Tubman lived for many years. She is buried there and honored by a tablet in the Cayuga County courthouse.

ROCK SCHOOL OR STANLEY INSTITUTE

Where: Near Cambridge on Rt. 16 where it intersects with Bayly Road
When: Open by request
Phone: 410-228-2875

On the southwestern edge of Cambridge, in what is known as the Christ Rock community, this little red schoolhouse became, in 1865, the first community-owned school in Dorchester County, and one of Maryland's first black community schools. It was named for Ezekiel Stanley, one of the community leaders who headed the effort. Twelve graduates became Methodist ministers on the Delmarva Peninsula.

The small, gable-roofed, one-story, frame structure is only twenty-nine feet by seventeen feet. It was used continuously for grades one through seven until July 15, 1966, when schools in Dorchester County were integrated.

William H. Kiah is one who attended and taught in the school and worked to preserve it as a museum. "There are about 106 museums in the United States devoted to Afro-American

Arresting in its simplicity, this little red schoolhouse was one of Maryland's first black community schools, now preserved as a museum.

history and culture," he explains, "but our museum is the only one of this type on the Eastern Shore. For a long time education was our main route to liberation. Now it is culture, religion, lifestyle, heritage, and all the questions that have to do with being. So we are saying who we are. The museums are responding to this need to define ourselves."

WILD GOOSE BREWERY

Where: At 20 Washington Street
When: Open Monday through Saturday, 10 a.m.
to 3 p.m.
Phone: 410-221-1121

The producers of Wild Goose Amber and Thomas Point Light beers offer tours (and free samples) to visitors to their micro-brewery Monday through Saturday from 10 a.m. to 3 p.m.

ALSO OF NOTE

"THE MOSQUITO"

The six-foot by eight-foot mosquito mounted on a pedestal in front of the Maryland Wire Belts, Inc. building in Church Creek was created out of scraps from the company's product, conveyor belts.

The company is located on Rt. 16 in the marshy Neck area west of Cambridge on the way to Blackwater National Wildlife Refuge. It does a thriving business weaving aluminum wire into spirals and other shapes for moving belts in canneries, packing houses, and similar industries.

Jim Vassar, a former employee now living in California, used to take home left-over aluminum wire to create his own original designs. One day about fifteen years ago, he came to the plant with the mosquito in the back of his pick-up truck.

It has become the emblem of the plant.

The six-foot by eight-foot mosquito at Church Creek seems just about life-size to summertime visitors to the Dorchester marshes.

To passersby who have experienced the mosquitoes that inhabit these marshes, this one would seem just about life-size.

OLD TRINITY CHURCH IN CHURCH CREEK

Where: South of Cambridge on Rt. 16

This little gem of a church, only twenty by thirty-eight feet with its semicircular apse, has been traced back to about 1675, making it the oldest church in America now in active use.

It was already here in its now isolated churchyard in Dorchester County's marshy countryside when the Establishment Act of 1692 created the original thirty Episcopal parishes in the Province of Maryland.

Over time, the building had been altered and was deteriorating. In the late 1950s, Colonel Edgar W. Garbish and his wife, Bernice, (both now deceased) sponsored an authentic restoration to stand as a memorial to her parents, Walter P. Chrysler, the automobile maker, and his wife, Della. Uncovered was the original floor of handmade bricks laid in sand on oyster shells. Heart pine was salvaged from old buildings to re-create the high box pews, unpainted and rubbed with beeswax. The Gothic lancet windows used in an 1850 alteration of the church were replaced by colonial style casement windows with clear leaded panes, and hand-woven hangings were reproduced.

The minuscule Old Trinity Church is said to be the oldest in America still in active use.

Outside, in a tree-shaded cemetery overlooking a tributary of Fishing Creek, is a Carroll family plot. It includes the graves of Thomas King

Carroll, an early governor of Maryland, and Anna Ella Carroll, a brilliant woman and military strategist who was friend, adviser, and ghost writer to Abraham Lincoln.

Visitor Center
Blackwater National Wildlife Refuge

Where: *Turn south on Rt. 16 east of Cambridge, then turn left at Church Creek on Rt. 335. Follow the signs to the refuge.*

When: *Wildlife Drive open daily, dawn to dusk. Visitor Center open daily, 7:30 a.m. to 4 p.m., Closed weekends June, July, and August. Closed Labor Day weekend*

Exhibits and films in the center relate to migratory waterfowl and the endangered species in the refuge—the bald eagle, Delmarva fox squirrel, and migrant peregrine falcon.

Outdoors, the peak season for visiting is in late October and November when the migrating ducks and Canada geese arrive. It is a pleasure to walk the trails in any season except midsummer, when the most overwhelming concentration here is not birds but flies and mosquitoes.

THE DORCHESTER MARSHES AND NARROWS FERRY BRIDGE

The traveler who ventures west of Cambridge into Dorchester County's lowlands and marshes will have the experience of lonely space and sudden surprises. One surprise is the concrete and steel bridge that curves twenty-seven feet above a fishing boat channel and looms like a mirage from two miles away across the empty marshes of Hoopers Island.

Hoopers Island is actually a chain of three islands between the Chesapeake Bay and the Honga River. They are occupied by about 750 people and four seafood houses. The bridge that connects the upper and lower islands cost $3.5 million to build, with the federal government paying seventy-five percent of the cost.

Its dedication in September 1980 made national news, reported by Walter Cronkite on the CBS Evening News. The reason for this unexpected attention was the invocation given by Thomas A. Flowers, a Dorchester County commissioner. It began, "Father, today we are gathered here to dedicate a bridge that is a monument to man's stupidity, a monument to man's waste, a monument to governmental interference and inefficiency."

While the surprised fellow commissioners and state and federal officials remained with heads bowed, Mr. Flowers continued, "For there is no need for such an elaborate structure as this is . . . which is so out of keeping in the peaceful and lovely environment of south Dorchester." He asked that the bridge be blessed even though, "wind and wave and tide are daily at work destroying that which has been built."

The islands on each side of the bridge are indeed eroding, but about 250 vehicles a day use it, including school buses. The old obsolete wooden drawbridge and its full-time tender are no more.

St. Mary's Star of the Sea at Golden Hill

Beyond Blackwater Wildlife Refuge on Rt. 335 toward Hoopers Island is a simple white frame structure so small it might be overlooked were it not for the historic marker beside it. It is a Roman Catholic chapel built in 1769 under the supervision of the Reverend Joseph Mosley, the Jesuit missionary who established the plantation Old St. Joseph's at Cordova. It is the third or fourth oldest Catholic church structure built in the English-speaking colonies.

The chapel was a church for 103 years. As the congregation grew, a new and bigger church was built, and the chapel sold to the school commissioners of Dorchester County. It was a school for fifty years and was then sold to a neighboring family who used it as a storage shed.

In 1960 it was bought and deeded back to the local Catholic church by a benefactor. It was restored as a historic shrine, with gifts from other private benefactors and the parish council.

An architectural history of Dorchester published by the Maryland Historical Trust describes both the chapel and the newer Gothic revival church across the road as being "imbued with a certain country sophistication."

THE BECKY PHIPPS CANNON

Where: By the Slaughter Creek Bridge, which connects Taylors Island to the mainland.

The cannon ensconced on a slab of concrete on this little-traveled waterfront was captured from the British in the War of 1812 by a company of volunteers from Taylors Island and nearby villages.

Local histories record that in the winter of 1814, the British warship, *Dauntless,* was based at Patuxent and was sending out tenders to forage for food from farms along the Eastern Shore. One of these, commanded by a Lieutenant Phipps, sailed up the Little Choptank River and got caught in drifting ice.

It was surrounded and captured by the local volunteers under the command of Captain Joseph Steward. The crew was taken prisoner, the ship dismantled, and the parts sold at auction. The cannon has been a proud symbol of the action ever since.

The Becky Phipps Cannon remains as a trophy of the War of 1812 in a waterfront village probably less traveled now than it was then.

It was nicknamed "Becky" for the cook who was captured with the British crew, and "Phipps" for the British lieutenant.

The cannon was fired on special occasions in the past, but it exploded when fired during a celebration of the election of Woodrow Wilson. It was later reassembled, mounted, and marked by the Daughters of the American Revolution.

TAYLORS ISLAND MUSEUM

Where: Reached by Rt. 16, about l5 miles west of Cambridge. Cross the Slaughter Creek bridge and bear right on Bayshore Road. Museum is on the left immediately past the firehouse.

When: Open by request
Phone: 410-397-3338 or 410-397-3262

The distinctive thing about the Taylors Island Museum is Taylors Island itself. This little community, located on a peninsula at the dead-end of Rt. 16, seems to be separated from the rest of the world by time and distance. Yet this was one of the first areas in Dorchester County to be settled. It was named for Thomas Taylor, one of the biggest early landowners. With its watery location and virgin forests, it became a shipbuilding center. Like other of the Shore's bayside villages, this one faded with the demise of waterborne commerce, leaving behind from that era only a few, fine, secluded eighteenth-century homes.

A hodgepodge of relics from the island's past are housed in an old, two-story, white frame schoolhouse, which is itself a relic. The school was built early in this century at a cost of $3,500. A square structure with six-pane sash windows like many another of its period in isolated Shore villages, it has three rooms and an auditorium.

When the school was closed in 1974, a local non-profit corporation called the Taylors Island Community Council acquired it from the county and created the museum with donations of money and display items. The collection is indiscriminate, and that is what gives it a special appeal. There are decorative items of the type found on Victorian mantlepieces, boat models, decoys, guns, muskrat traps, fossil bones, and Indian arrowheads.

Its premier exhibit is a model of Spocot Windmill. The reconstructed mill, described on page 97, is worth another stop in a tour of Dorchester's marshy necks.

DORCHESTER HERITAGE MUSEUM AT HORN POINT

Where: *About 3½ miles west of Cambridge. Follow Rt. 343 for about 2 miles bearing right at a fork onto Horn Point Road. Continue for 1½ miles. The museum is in a former airplane hanger on the property of the University of Maryland Center for Environmental and Estuarine Studies.*

When: *Open April 15 through October 30, Saturday and Sunday: 1 p.m. to 4:30 p.m.*

Phone: *800-522-TOUR or 410-228-1000*

The Dorchester Heritage Museum began as a project of the South Dorchester High School graduating class of 1970 under an imaginative teacher, Morley Jull. Its theme is "A Walk Through Time." It brings local history to life with exhibits that begin with geologic time—giant scallop shells, sharks' teeth, and whale bones recovered from layers of soil where

The Dorchester Heritage Museum in a former private airplane hanger developed from a high school student project into an engrossing museum for all comers.

they were left eons ago as the Chesapeake Bay and Choptank River evolved.

There are pottery shards and arrowheads from hundreds of years of Indian habitation, artifacts that seem to be especially abundant along the shorelines of Dorchester rivers. Exhibits in lighted cases with beautifully printed and worded explanations beside each lead the visitor through daily life from colonial settlement to the early twentieth century. There are watermen's tools that look historic but are, in some cases, still used on Dorchester County rivers and coves, re-creating the early days of familiar local businesses.

The museum is supported and maintained by volunteers organized as Dorchester Heritage, Inc.

SPOCOT WINDMILL

Where: On Rt. 343 about 6 miles west of Cambridge
When: Open daily for self-guided tours
Phone: 410-228-7090

The authentically reproduced Spocot Windmill is what is known as a "post mill" and is the only one of its kind in Maryland. It is operated by canvas sails with a wingspan of fifty-two feet. They are attached to a red board-and-batten house that rests on a post and turns with the wind. The wide sails turn a wooden shaft and a series of wooden gears that turn the upper millstone, grinding the grain.

The original mill had been blown down in a storm in 1888. It stood on property that has been in the Radcliffe family since 1662. The late Senator George C. Radcliffe remembered it from childhood. Senator Radcliffe was the benefactor of many a historical preservation project in Dorchester County and the reconstruction was conceived as a project in his memory.

Spocot Windmill could stand as well as a memorial to the remarkable man who built it— the late James B. Richardson, master shipwright and neighbor of Senator

Spocot Windmill, the only one of its kind in Maryland, is a re-creation that memorializes not only Senator George C. Radcliffe, on whose property it stands, but also James B. Richardson, the master shipwright who built it.

Radcliffe. "Mr. Jim," as he was known here and afar, was a builder of the traditional wooden workboats of Chesapeake Bay, probably best known for reproductions of Maryland's *Dove* and South Carolina's seventeenth-century ketch, *Adventure*.

The Spocot property, with its rambling white frame plantation house, is now owned and occupied by George M. Radcliffe Sr., a lawyer active in both the state and local historical societies.

In the eighteenth century, the house was the center of a cluster of buildings that made the plantation a community in itself. To recapture that period, the family and friends who organized Spocot Windmill Foundation, Inc.' have restored and furnished a 1½-story farmhouse dated about 1800 and the 1870 Castle Haven one-room school that, according to the Maryland Historical Trust, "easily stands as one of the best such structures in the state."

There is no guide on hand except by special arrangement. The buildings speak for themselves and are open for visitors to explore on their own. In spite of Spocot's remote location, visitors in surprising numbers come here year round.

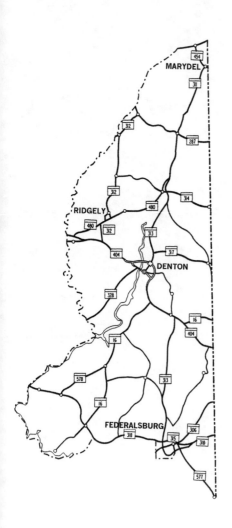

CAROLINE COUNTY

CAROLINE COUNTY

*S*ince vacationers are drawn as if by gravity to waterfronts, Caroline, the Shore's only inland county, is a place to pass through to get to the ocean beaches. For those who know better, it offers bass fishing, canoeing, and seclusion at two state parks, Martinak on the upper Choptank, and Tuckahoe on the scenic river of that name. Both are reached off of Rt. 404, Tuckahoe west of Denton and Martinak east of it.

Denton itself invites a stop with its newly developed Caroline County Museum.

CAROLINE COUNTY MUSEUM OF RURAL LIFE

Where: On the Court House Green in Denton
When: Open by appointment
Phone: 410-479-1750

Caroline County Museum began, as have others in towns across the Shore, with the threatened demolition of a late eighteenth-century house embodying in its past much of the history of this farm-centered community.

The Annie Taylor House, as it is known, dates to 1795. It was moved four blocks to its new site, an achievement in itself, and renovated as money could be raised. It is a small two-story frame house with lovely paneling inside and is now being used for courthouse-related receptions and similar affairs.

A separate wing has been added for a developing museum for artifacts and oral histories centering on the county's farm life from the glory days of the grain boom in the early nineteenth century to the agricultural depression at the century's close, to the era of truck crops and canneries to today's grain and poultry economy.

A lot of research is going into this museum. Its planned audio-visual presentation should make it unique among the Shore's small museums.

CHESAPEAKE RAILROAD EXCURSION TRAIN

Where: At Central Avenue and the Railroad in Ridgely
When: For current schedule, call 410-482-2330
and . . . Ticket fee

Beginning in the summer of 1995 with what was called "Six Months of Sundays," the newly activated railroad offered ten-mile excursions to the rural town of Queen Anne and back on the last Sunday of the month from June to November. The success of the venture promised an expanded schedule now in effect.

This line is a segment of one of the earliest Eastern Shore railroad ventures, the Maryland and Delaware Railroad, chartered in Maryland on May 10, 1854, to run from Clayton, Delaware, to Oxford, Maryland. General Tench Tilghman, grandson of the Revolutionary War hero of the same name, invested and lost much money in this project, which was interrupted by the Civil War. The town of Ridgely was founded because of the railroad and named for the Reverend G. W. Ridgely who lived nearby. By the time it reached Oxford in 1871, the initial investors had lost it for debts.

The line eventually became part of the Pennsylvania Railroad and then the Penn Central system before being taken over by the state of Maryland. The segment from Ridgely to Queen Anne has now been acquired as a private venture—with much enthusiasm—by Bill Bartosh.

For the passenger excursions, he uses a vintage diesel engine and three cars, including a 1912 Pullman car. He offers it also for private charters, luncheons, and dinners. It rolls through farmland, woodland, and across bridges—"Nature at its best," says Mr. Bartosh.

ADKINS ARBORETUM

Where: *In Tuckahoe Park. Turn north off of Rt. 404 near Hillsboro onto Rt. 480 and then immediately to the left onto Eveland Road. The visitor center is visible to the left about 2 miles beyond.*

When: *Grounds open daily March through October, 9 a.m. to 5 p.m. Closed weekends, November through February*

Phone: *410-634-2847*

Adkins Arboretum is one of the least known Shore destinations in one of Maryland's quietest state parks—Tuckahoe. The arboretum includes about 425 acres of the extensive park along Tuckahoe Creek, which forms a meandering border between Queen Anne's and Caroline Counties. It

includes swamp-
land along the
creek, upland
forest, some pine
plantation, sec-
ond growth for-
est, and sandy
meadowlands.

*Adkins Arboretum, with a visitor center
and several miles of trails and footpaths,
is an adventure awaiting discovery,
covering 425 acres of Tuckahoe
State Park.*

There is a
visitor center
with exhibition
lobby and small
auditorium.
Leading from
the center are
three miles of graded trails with wooden foot-
bridges across swampy areas and more miles of
footpaths branching off.

There has been some mixed forest planting
along the loop trails, with more planned—par-
ticularly ornamental plantings of native species
around the visitor center. The use of native plants
for landscaping and the protection of biological
diversity are two of the thrusts of the arboretum.

The Adkins Arboretum was conceived by the
late Leon Andrus of Cheston-on-Wye near
Queenstown. He endowed it, asked that it be
named in honor of the Adkins family that has produced civic leaders on the Shore for generations,

and set up a non-profit corporation called Friends of the Adkins Arboretum.

The project developed over several years with support from the Maryland Department of Natural Resources. In March 1995 it was reorganized, with the Friends negotiating a property lease from the state and taking on the support and management of the arboretum independently.

The visitor center will surprise the unknowing visitor with its attractive rustic design and landscaping and the exhibits inside that introduce the native plant communities to adults and children alike. There are brochures identifying the plants and birds to be seen along the trails, which are an adventure in any season.

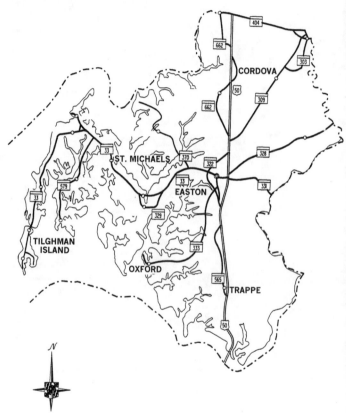

TALBOT COUNTY

TALBOT COUNTY

*F*or the Eastern Shore visitor by bicycle, car, or tour bus, the most popular destination is the thirty-mile circuit through three historic Talbot County towns—Easton, Oxford and St. Michaels.

From Easton, one continues to St. Michaels by Route 33, or to Oxford by Route 333. The loop is joined by a crossing of the Tred Avon River on the Oxford-Bellevue Ferry. In all three towns, the restaurants, overnight accommodations, and historic attractions are so numerous that the only problems are choice and, at the height of the season, crowds.

EASTON

MONUMENT TO "THE TALBOT BOYS" AT THE TALBOT COUNTY COURTHOUSE IN EASTON

Although Easton's mystique is colonial or early American, the hero of the past immortalized on the courthouse lawn is a Confederate soldier embracing the flag of the Lost Cause.

"To the Talbot Boys—1861–1865—C.S.A." reads the inscription on the pedestal. On its sides

A Confederate soldier embraces the flag of the Lost Cause on the Talbot County courthouse lawn in Easton.

are the names of eighty-five men who fought for the Confederacy with an additional eleven listed as "Citizens After War."

Actually, most of this area's fighting men fought for the Union. When the monument was erected in 1915–16, however, Civil War passions were still strong and the county was dominated by Southern sympathizers. A proposal to dedicate the monument to both sides was turned down.

Among the Confederate heroes named on the monument

are some names that stand out. There is Admiral Franklin Buchanan who had served as the first commandant of the United States Naval Academy at Annapolis from 1845 to 1847 before resigning his commission to join the Confederate Navy. He survived the war and ended his life at his estate on the Miles River.

Two Confederate brigadier generals are named. General Charles S. Winder was right-hand man to Thomas "Stonewall" Jackson and was killed at the Battle of Cedar Mountain in 1862. General Lloyd Tilghman was killed at Vicksburg in 1863 and is memorialized by an equestrian statue in the Vicksburg National Military Park.

At Gettysburg, a Confederate regiment and a Union regiment of Talbot boys fought and killed each other at Culp's Hill where both regiments are honored by monuments.

A local historian has written that the secessionist side in the struggle between the states was "the fashionable side" to be on in Easton and "a pass-port to select social circles."

On the southeast corner of the courthouse lawn stands a more recent memorial, a reminder of another of this nation's tragic wars. It honors ten Talbot County men who died in Vietnam between 1968 and 1973. The inscription on their monument reads, "If you forget my death then I have died in vain."

ACADEMY OF THE ARTS

Where: At South and Harrison Streets
When: Open Monday through Saturday, 10 a.m. to
4 p.m. Closed in August
Phone: 410-822-0455

Vitality and creativity are as evident on walking into Easton's Academy of the Arts as the imaginative architecture. Behind the modest facade of an 1820s schoolhouse with its distinctive bell tower, the door opens into a bright and airy two-story atrium.

Both the entrance atrium and the galleries that open from it feature with equal prominence a permanent collection and special exhibitions of professional artists, and the colorful and uninhibited drawings, paintings, paper sculpture, and ceramics of children. The academy offers more than 130 low-cost and free classes in visual and performing arts to young people in three counties.

In studios on two floors, young people and adults are learning how to do watercolors, use the potter's wheel, play guitar, or move with basic ballet techniques.

The visitor will catch one or two of the twenty-four exhibitions featured each year in its galleries.

In the courtyard off the atrium, the centerpiece is the bronze figure of an oysterman with an actual set of tongs. In the front yard is the bronze bust of the late Lee Lawrie, a local resident and internationally renowned sculptor who was one of the initiators of the Academy in 1958.

The bust is the work of Joseph Kiselowski of New York, a former student of Mr. Lawrie. Lee Lawrie was brought to this country as an infant from Rixdorf, Germany. He was to become one of the great architectural sculptors of his day, probably best known for his Atlas at Rockefeller Center in New York.

At the unveiling of the bust at the Academy of the Arts in 1976, friends recounted such personal memories of the artist as the sixty-four cats that obstructed their passage when visiting his home at Locust Lane Farm near Easton.

The arts center he helped found for his adopted town today has a professional staff of five, more than forty trustees, and innumerable volunteers. Its considerable budget comes from memberships, contributions, and grants from the Maryland State Arts Council and the separate arts councils of three Eastern Shore counties.

If there can be a tangible demonstration of the arts as a center of community life, this is it.

Museum Complex of the Historical Society of Talbot County

Where: At 25 South Washington Street
When: Open Tuesday through Saturday, 10 a.m. to
4 p.m.; Sunday, 1 p.m. to 4 p.m. Daily
walking tour of the Historic District by group
reservation, 11:30 a.m. and 1:30 p.m.
Phone: 410-822-0773
and . . . Entry fee

In Talbot County it is the newcomer as much
as the native who has a passion for the past. Attesting to this are the more than 1,400 members
who make the Talbot County Historical Society
the biggest county society in the state.

In a burst of acquisition a few years ago, the
society expanded its holdings in downtown Easton
to eight historic structures in a three-block area. A
handsome Federal period townhouse, the Neall
House, has been the society headquarters since
1956. Beside it an addition for offices and special
exhibits was built in 1978 behind an existing traditional storefront.

The two buildings are linked by a garden designed and tended by the Talbot County Garden
Club. Walkways through the garden lead to three
small houses that have been moved to the property for preservation. One was the story-and-a-half

shop and home of an eighteenth-century cabinet maker. A second 1825 dwelling is rented and occupied. A third, called "The Ending of Controversie," was the seventeenth-century home of a Talbot County Quaker pioneer and was a gift to the society by Dr. H. Chandlee Forman, an art educator, architect, and archaeologist who had reconstructed the original. It contains his personal collection of folk art and artifacts.

The Talbot County Historical Society, the biggest local society in the state, maintains historic structures in a three-block area in Easton.

Across a municipal parking lot a former nineteenth-century Methodist Church was acquired by the society and renovated with office space for rent at street level and a three hundred-seat auditorium for community use upstairs.

On the other side of the street, the society acquired an early nineteenth-century Federal period townhouse known as the Tharpe House and turned it into a museum shop. Next door to that the Jenkins House awaits a future use.

There is no question that Easton and Talbot County have a mystique that brings many a visitor to the renowned Tidewater Inn in the heart of the downtown. If the visitor strolls past the inviting shops and well-tended gardens to the complex on south Washington Street, he will not be disappointed.

AVALON THEATER

Where: *At 40 East Dover Street across from the*
          Tidewater Inn
When: *Open for special events*
Phone: *410-822-0345*

There is generally something going on at the Avalon Theater on weekends—a surprising array of things. Most surprising of all is to discover art deco preserved on an intimate scale in the heart of Easton, a community as conscious of its colonial- and Federal-period architecture and heritage as any on the Shore.

The Avalon was built in 1921 and restored in 1989. It is small but marvelously gaudy. Its rebirth was achieved by a non-profit foundation as a setting for community events, private affairs, concerts, films—whatever. In the spring of 1995, for example, it was used for a performance by the Easton High School Drama Club; a choral cantata for the Easter season; an old-fashioned live radio variety show aired over a local public radio station; an Earth Day celebration; a Cinema Arts series; a United States Navy chorus called The Sea Chanters; and rock, bluegrass, and chamber music groups.

When in town, take the time to check it out.

THIRD HAVEN MEETING

Where: On South Washington Street

Third Haven Meeting was built in 1682 and has been in continuous use since. It is the oldest frame church building in the United States.

George Fox, founder of the Quaker movement in England, came to Maryland in the early 1670s and helped organize the Third Haven Meeting when he visited

Third Haven Meeting in Easton is said to be the oldest frame church building in the United States.

the Easton area in 1673. On his return to England, he sent a number of books to the Meeting, thereby starting what some regard as the first public library in Talbot County, and maybe the province.

William Penn preached in this Meeting House in 1700 to an assemblage from both sides of the bay, including the state's most prominent Catholics, Lord and Lady Baltimore and their party.

Old Third Haven is at the end of a driveway lined with stately oaks. The timbers were hewn with a broadax, the marks of which are visible on the rafters.

THE RUINS OF OLD WHITEMARSH

The ruins of this church, only two hundred yards from U.S. 50 between Easton and Trappe, are more striking to the passing motorist than the new and active churches. Whitemarsh was one of the earliest Episcopal parish churches on the Shore. It served the eastern part of Talbot County around Oxford and Easton. It has been given several dates, the most authoritative being 1685. A brush fire in 1897 reduced it to ruins and it was never rebuilt.

A group called the Old Whitemarsh Cemetery Association has acquired the site and in 1976 stabilized the ruins and restored the cemetery for continued use. The Talbot County Committee of the Maryland House and Garden Pilgrimage beautified the grounds with plantings along a brick walkway and other touches.

It makes a pleasant pause for the passerby. Among the graves in the cemetery is that of Robert Morris Sr., father of the financier of the American Revolution. He was killed in 1750 at the age of forty when wounded by a wad from a cannon fired by a ship in Oxford harbor in his honor.

OXFORD

OXFORD MUSEUM

Where: *Behind the Town Office at Morris and Market Streets*
When *Open mid-April through October, Friday through Sunday: 2 p.m. to 5 p.m.*
Phone: *410-226-5331*

Oxford is changing around the edges. It is encircled with new houses whose builders are all trying to be part of the old established town. Oxford has a charm that is hard to define. As the new developments demonstrate, it is a charm that cannot be acquired overnight.

The Oxford Museum seems but an extension of the heritage and special character of the town that is visible along its streets. The displays relate to Oxford's colonial days as a prosperous commercial port, and to its heroes of Revolutionary War days—Robert Morris (the inn at the end of the street is named for him), father of the Robert Morris of Philadelphia known as the financier of the American Revolution; Jeremiah Banning, sea captain and patriot; and Lt. Col. Tench Tilghman, George Washington's aide de camp. There are also tools, ship models, and marine engines related to the town's later days as a community of watermen, seafood packers, and boat builders.

Today the strolling sightseers in the streets and the visitors to this museum are part of another transformation of the town into a pleasure-boating center for racing yachts and that distinctive craft of the Chesapeake, the racing log canoe; a tourists' destination; and home to buyers from out of the area willing to pay prices for real estate undreamed of by the watermen who once lived and worked here.

OXFORD CUSTOMS HOUSE

Where: *At Morris Street and The Strand*
When: *Open mid-April to mid-October, Saturday and Sunday: 3 p.m. to 5 p.m.*
Phone: *410-226-5760*

The tiny one-room frame structure overlooking Oxford's Strand is a replica of the first United States customs house established here by the new nation in the 1790s and representing a turning point in the town's history. It was a Bicentennial project of the town's citizens.

In 1694 Oxford had been designated a port of entry, meaning that this Eastern Shore town and Annapolis across the bay were the sole official ports for the Maryland province. As the clouds of revolution gathered, one of the first moves of the Continental Congress, meeting in Philadelphia, was to impose an embargo on all trade with Britain. Thus, on September 11, 1775, the last British vessel was recorded in Port of Oxford records and the town's days of commercial greatness were over.

A replica of the Oxford Customs House, established here by the new nation in the 1790s, was a Bicentennial project of the town's citizens.

During the eight years of war, Oxford's port was all but deserted and its merchants departed.

At the war's close, Jeremiah Banning, one of the town's heroes, a ship captain, patriot, and friend of George Washington, was appointed by the nation's first president to be United States Collector of Customs for the Port of Oxford. The captain was then sixty years old and suffering acutely from gout. He retired to The Isthmus, his home across the Tred Avon River from the town. It was here that he built a one-room customs house on the lawn of his home, thereby obliging ship captains to row across the river to pay their duties. The original customs house remains on a private lawn at The Isthmus today.

The replica customs house on Oxford's Strand was a project headed by two of Oxford's most prominent citizens two hundred years later, Mary Hanks and the late Bertha S. Adkins, assistant secretary of Health, Education and Welfare under President Eisenhower. The house looks out over a harbor known to pleasure-sailors around the world. The port Oxford might have become is now Baltimore.

THE COOPERATIVE OXFORD LAB

Where: At 904 S. Morris Street at street's dead-end
When: Tours Monday through Friday, 1 p.m. to 2 p.m.
No appointment necessary

The National Marine Fisheries Service and the Maryland Department of Natural Resources cooperate at this lab in research into the complexities of the fish and shellfish of Chesapeake Bay and the causes of, and remedies for, the diseases that afflict them.

Visitors are taken through the histology unit where biologists peer through microscopes at the tissues of oysters and other sea creatures; through the immunology department where scientists study the responses of sea life to various phenomena; to the Beachhouse where tanks of fish are kept for the study of health and disease; and to the inevitable computer room where fish, oysters, and other bay life are mapped and analyzed. Of particular interest is the lab's study of stranded marine mammals—dolphins, seals, whales, or sea turtles—that are brought here to try to find a cause of death.

Even if the visitor is not into the nitty-gritties of scientific research, a tour of the lab is illuminating in its demonstration that the relationship between man and his environment is not a simple one to be dismissed or belittled with uninformed clichés.

THE OXFORD-BELLEVUE FERRY

The ferry across the Tred Avon River has operated since 1683, although with not quite the same usage that it has today. It is now, as it was then, a privately owned and operated ferry, but its prosperity today is as a tourist attraction. A crossing of the Tred Avon is part of the appeal of the Easton-Oxford-St. Michaels circuit. About thirty thousand cars a year ride this ferry. Visitors pay $3.50 for the ten-minute crossing, catching glimpses of osprey, log canoes under sail, and waterfront estates on the way.

The first operator over three centuries ago was paid twenty-five hundred pounds of tobacco a year by the Talbot County Court for a ferry service. It was out of business for sixty years after the American Revolution, but has been in continuous operation since 1836. The latest operator replaced the long running three-car ferry first with a six-car vessel and then with a ten-car steel ferry to handle the ever-increasing traffic.

ST. MICHAELS

CHESAPEAKE BAY MARITIME MUSEUM

Where: *On Navy Point, marked by a sign on Talbot Street (Rt. 33)*

When: *Open summer, Sunday through Friday: 10 a.m. to 5 p.m.; Saturday, 10 a.m. to 7 p.m. Open mid-March to summer and September to January, 10 a.m. to 4 p.m. Open January to mid-March week-ends and holidays, 10 a.m. to 4 p.m. Closed on Christmas, New Year's, and Thanksgiving*

Phone: *410-745-2916*

and . . . Entry fee

In May 1965 the Chesapeake Bay Maritime Museum opened in three houses on the harbor of

St. Michaels. The dedication ceremony drew one thousand people. It was a triumph for the volunteers who had worked for two years to bring it about as a project of the Historical Society of Talbot County.

Today the museum has become the major Eastern Shore attraction with excursion boats at its harbor, a stream of tourist buses, and license plates from across the nation in its extensive parking lots.

It is a private, non-profit institution and has expanded into a complex of eighteen separate structures, a year-round staff of twenty-five and summertime staff of thirty-five, an annual operating budget of $650,000, and 100,000 visitors a year.

A floating fleet of classic bay workboats is maintained on the museum's own marine railway and kept sailing by experienced staff and volunteers.

There are a Small Boat Exhibit Shed where wooden craft

St. Michaels' Chesapeake Bay Maritime Museum, the Eastern Shore's biggest and probably best known museum, is a complex of eighteen separate structures, including this lighthouse and bell tower, and has a floating fleet of classic Bay workboats.

span the bay's history from the single log canoe of a York River Indian; exhibits related to the

development of the Baltimore clippers, steamboat days, the oysterman, and waterfowling; a bell tower that once signaled ships from Point Lookout; a gazebo bandstand from Tolchester Beach in the days of excursion boats from Baltimore; and the old Hooper's Strait Lighthouse. It is not a fast-walk-through kind of place.

The famous figurehead at St. Michaels

The museum has transformed St. Michaels from a simple, working seafood harbor to a destination for pleasure boaters and sightseers and a harbor surrounded by restaurants, new condominiums, and high-priced real estate.

Because this is by far the biggest and most widely acclaimed of the Shore's museums, it epitomizes the way the region is changing. It preserves and idealizes a way of life that is loved by artists, photographers, and those who go down to the sea by pleasure boat or book. But the watermen who actually live this life are already far outnumbered by the visitors who view their occupation, its tools and craft as colorful atmosphere and seek seafood on waterfronts where fewer and fewer fish are being landed.

St. Mary's Square Museum

*Where: On "The Green," around which St. Michaels
was originally built*

*When: Open May through October, Saturday and
Sunday: 10 a.m. to 4 p.m.*

Besides maintaining this museum with its artifacts and documents from the town's long and colorful past, St. Mary's Square Museum, Inc. has identified the historic homes and buildings of St. Michaels with small bronze plaques. A brochure is available at the museum and elsewhere in town outlining a walking tour for the visitor.

The museum itself got underway in 1964 when a committee organized to save one of the town's oldest houses from demolition for commercial development. The house was moved to this pleasant square and restored. A second house, also threatened with destruction, was later attached to the first.

This small museum on St. Mary's Square, hidden from the bustle of the Maritime Museum in the heart of historic St. Michaels, displays artifacts and documents from the town's long and colorful past.

The shotgun over the mantel, the rustic bedroom upstairs, the wooden farm tools and kitchen utensils give this small museum a warm and homey feel. Here also is the stark realism of life in a watermen's town—the "carrying board" for transporting drowned bodies from the water.

Because this town was a boatbuilding center, producing privateers and blockade runners as well as the famed Baltimore Clippers, it was a target for the British in the War of 1812. Its most cherished story is of the townspeople hanging lanterns in the trees to misguide the British cannonfire, a story explaining its recurring identity here as "The Town That Fooled The British."

A seal designed for the museum according to the rules and language of heraldry has become the official flag of St. Michaels. It features the sword of the biblical Archangel St. Michael, the name of the Episcopal parish that was established here in 1677 and gave the town its name.

MUSEUM OF COSTUME

Where: At 400 St. Mary's Square
When: Open by appointment April through November, 11 a.m. to 5 p.m.
Phone: 410-745-5154
and . . . Entry fee

The first surprise at this private museum in the heart of historic St. Michaels is that it has nothing to do with boats, watermen, or the lore of the Shore. It has to do with the life-long obsession of the collector, Millie B. Curtis, with clothes.

The second surprise is the stunning result of her obsession. The thousands of items in her collection—elaborately stitched gowns, coats, gloves, muffs, impossibly narrow and delicate shoes, boas, fans, parasols, buckles, and bows—cover fashion from the early 1800s into the 1960s. Some have a celebrity connection—the shimmering dress worn in the 1920s by Natasha Rambova, second wife of Rudolph Valentino … a deep rose gold-threaded dress worn by Greta Garbo.

In one room, scores of feathered and beribboned hats line the walls. In a Children's Room, doll-like mannequins wear linen suits and delicate little girl dresses from the days when they were lovingly embroidered in white on white. There is a room labeled Ladies' Hidden Luxury, with lingerie in clouds of silk, satin, and fur.

Unrelated to local color but with a lot of color of its own, the Museum of Costume—in a one-time captain's house on St. Mary's Square—houses a stunning private collection of clothing and accessories from the early 1800s into the 1960s.

Mrs. Curtis grew up in a small town in North Carolina, one of fourteen children. As a young bride she went to Washington with her husband, owner of the old Pennsylvania Hotel there, and discovered "a whole new lifestyle." As a widow, she moved in 1985 to St. Michaels, a town he loved, and bought a house on historic St. Mary's Square that had been the home of a sea captain. Because it is unrelated to the maritime tradition of the town and has attracted tour buses to its quiet neighborhood, her museum has not been altogether welcome by some of the local populace. All the same, most visitors will be enthralled, especially with Millie Curtis as a guide, bringing her collection to glowing life. Her love for it is contagious. "At night I like to just walk through these rooms with the lights dimmed," she said.

ALSO OF NOTE

OLD ST. JOSEPH'S AT CORDOVA

Where: On Rt. 309 north of Easton

The present St. Joseph's dates back to 1782, making it the second oldest Roman Catholic church building in continuous use in America.

(The oldest is St. Mary's in Philadelphia, built in 1763.) It was part of a mission of the Jesuit plantation at Old Bohemia farther north near Warwick. Father Joseph Mosely acquired two hundred and seven acres near Cordova and established the mission in 1765. It was his responsibility to meet the spiritual needs of parishioners scattered over a wide countryside and to build the mission complex and manage the plantation to support it.

One section of the church building that stands today was a brick dwelling built by Father Mosely. The present sanctuary is the chapel that he built. The clover-leaf apse was added in 1903.

Father Mosely is buried under the church floor, as are three other early priests.

LONGWOOD SCHOOL, "THE LITTLE RED SCHOOLHOUSE"

Where: *On Rt. 662 (Longwoods Road)*
When: *Visits by appointment; call Talbot County Department of Parks and Recreation*
Phone: *410-822-2955*

This last remaining one-room school in Talbot County was built in 1887 at a cost of $1,215. It replaced an older one that was sold at auction for $190. It was described in the builder's contract at the time as being twenty-four feet by forty-six feet with a back shed for fuel. Sometimes it was referred to as the Germantown school because of some families from Germany and Prussia who had moved into the area and whose children attended it.

The little school has been preserved as the last of its era in the county and a tribute to public education of the not too distant past.

WYE MILL

Where: On Rt. 662 just off U.S. 50, 15 miles east of
the Bay Bridge
When: Open weekends April 1 through October 31,
11 a.m. to 4 p.m. Group tours by appointment.
Phone: 410-827-6909 or 410-685-2886

It seems perfectly natural for the old Wye Mill to be working in Wye Mills, a haven of the past just off a teeming twentieth-century highway. Just up the road is Maryland's state tree, the four-hundred-year-old Wye Oak, and beside it the still active eighteenth-century Old Wye Church.

There has been a grist mill at work here for over three hundred years. During the American Revolution, the mill was run by Colonel William Hemsley, who filled an order placed by Robert

Morris, the Revolution's financier, for wheat meal for the Continental Army at Valley Forge.

The mill's last commercial miller, Winthrop Blakeslee, retired in 1951. When the mill dam washed out during Hurricane Connie in 1953, the state of Maryland bought the mill, the dam, the pond, and sixty-four acres and redammed the Wye East

With a new metal overshot wheel and hydro system, the grinding stones of Old Wye Mill are again turned by water power as they were when they ground wheat for the Continental Army at Valley Forge.

River to create the present fifty-acre lake. The pond, part of a flood control project, is used by fishermen and feeds the mill race.

In 1956 the state deeded the mill to Preservation Maryland, a private non-profit organization. With financial help from Arthur A. Houghton Jr., who also restored Old Wye Church nearby, the deteriorating mill was restored with new siding and shingles.

In 1971 it reopened for several years, run by students at nearby Chesapeake College as part of a work-study program.

Until the fall of 1988, it was operated by an electrically driven pair of millstones. To get it operating again with water power required new equipment. Preservation Maryland organized a Wye Mill Restoration committee to raise the money.

In July of 1989 a new metal overshot wheel and hydro system were installed to turn the one-hundred-year-old grinding stones. Visitors can see it in operation every third Saturday from April through October.

On other weekends, it is worth a stop for exhibits down among its wooden gears and shafts, tracing the history of this area's grain farming from the wheat boom of 1790 through 1830 to the Shore's big poultry conglomerates of today.

OLD WYE CHURCH

Where: Off U.S. 50 on Rt. 662

Old Wye Church has stood in its grove of huge oaks, sisters of the famed Wye Oak nearby, since 1721. It was then a chapel of ease in an Upper Shore parish of the Anglican Church in Maryland. It survived the Revolutionary War period despite the division of loyalties among its parishioners.

After the war, communicants and revenue for this and other of the Shore's Church of England parishes nearly vanished. It was rescued from oblivion in 1854 after a visiting bishop from Baltimore happened to pass by with his party, found it being used as a stable with cattle inside, and initiated its restoration.

In the early part of this century, it again fell into decline until rescued by Arthur A. Houghton Jr., who had purchased the nearby Wye Plantation. Under his benefaction, the restoration was directed by William G. Perry, supervising architect for Colonial Williamsburg. It was completed in 1949.

It now has a full-time rector and supportive congregation.

For the traveler, it can be a pleasant stop that also includes the small park surrounding the Wye Oak, Maryland's state tree, and the restored Old Wye Mill.

UPPER SHORE

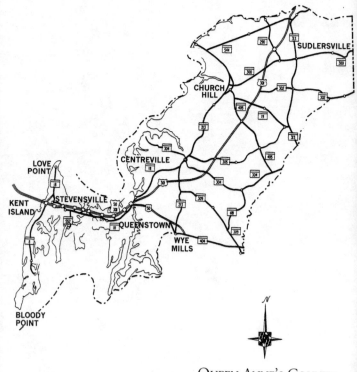

QUEEN ANNE'S COUNTY

QUEEN ANNE'S COUNTY

*T*he three Upper Shore counties stretching along the bay north of the Chesapeake Bay Bridge combine expanses of well-tended farmland, waterfronts, and wooded shorelines protected by environmental easements. To drive north or south along Rt. 213 or the dual but lightly traveled U.S. 301 is to enjoy some of Maryland's most pleasant countryside.

Driving eastward across the Bay Bridge, the motorist enters the Shore across Kent Island, which is in Queen Anne's County and not to be confused with Kent County farther north. Kent Island has become an extension of suburbia with a commuter population heading daily for Annapolis, Washington, or Baltimore. It is only when one reaches Kent Narrows with its marinas, rows of workboats, and seafood restaurants that the storied Shore begins to emerge.

As one heads north, almost any byway is worth exploring (with the help of a Maryland map available at any State Police headquarters). The museums, churches, and historic sites here described are destinations that might give direction and purpose to the exploration.

KENT ISLAND

THE CRAY HOUSE AT STEVENSVILLE AND STEVENSVILLE TRAIN STATION

Where: *On Cockey's Lane*
When: *Open May through October, Saturday: 1 p.m. to 4 p.m.; or by request*
Phone: *410-827-4810*

Kent Island's heritage isn't entirely buried by new development. The island became the site of the oldest English-speaking settlement in Maryland when Captain William Claiborne sailed up Chesapeake Bay from Virginia in 1631 and established a trading post here. This was three years before Leonard Calvert landed at St. Clement's Island with the *Ark* and the *Dove*.

Documents attesting to this fact are on display at Cray House, headquarters of the Kent Island Heritage Society. The society was organized and the house restored as a Bicentennial project.

The Cray House, with its gambrel roof and rustic interior, is the headquarters of the Kent Island Heritage Society and a symbol of the island's celebrated past.

Likewise on display are scrapbooks of clippings and photographs of two major events in 1981 that celebrated the island's origins. The first, that April, was a visit by The Most Reverend Robert A. K. Runcie, Lord Archbishop of Canterbury and titular head of the worldwide Anglican community. Archbishop Runcie participated in two services commemorating the 350th anniversary of the island's Christ Church parish, which began with Captain Claiborne's settlement. It is thus recognized as the oldest parish in continuous existence in Maryland and one of the oldest in the nation. With Archbishop Runcie on that occasion was Terry Waite, whose name was later to be known around the world as one of the hostages of terrorists in Lebanon.

At a second celebration that August, a pageant dramatized the settlement of Captain Claiborne and his defeat in a naval engagement by the forces of Leonard Calvert.

The Cray House is the oldest house in Stevensville. It is distinguished by a rustic interior and the simple life it represents. It is a gambrel-roofed wood frame house. The oldest part is of a post-and-plank construction described by an architect-historian as "exceedingly rare or possibly unique." Stairsteps almost as narrow as a ladder lead to three upstairs bedrooms, one opening into the other with no hallway between. Donors have supplied one-hundred-year-old quilts for the bedsteads.

The house was a gift to the Heritage Society in 1976 by the heirs of Nora Cray, a widow with nine children who bought it at auction in 1914.

On the grounds beside it, the original Stevensville train station built in 1902 has been moved and restored with a related mural and model train on display. It is a reminder of the impact of the railroad on the island until its demise was heralded by one of its last loads, materials for the construction of the original span of the Bay Bridge in 1952.

The Stevensville Train Station

The Heritage Society has continued to celebrate the island's past with two annual events:

Kent Island Days the third weekend in May, and a walking tour of Old Stevensville the first Sunday in December.

KENT ISLAND FEDERATION OF ART

Where: At 405 Main Street in Stevensville
When: Open Tuesday through Thursday, 1 p.m. to 4 p.m.; Saturday, noon to 4 p.m.
Phone: 410-643-7424 for information on current shows

The center for the arts in one of this small town's period homes has been active for over two decades. It has rotating exhibits.

ALSO OF NOTE

THE WILDFOWL TRUST OF NORTH AMERICA AT HORSEHEAD WETLANDS CENTER

Where: Reached by turning south at Grasonville off of Rt. 18 onto Perry Corner Road. The well-marked lane is on the right, about ½ mile down the road.
When: Open daily, 9 a.m. to 5 p.m.
and . . . Entry fee

An hour a day could be spent on the trails, in the observation blinds and towers, or along the boardwalk or canoe trail on this 310-acre former hunting property now dedicated "to the preservation of wildfowl and wetlands through conservation, education, research, and recreation." It is a great place to bring children (but no pets).

More than a mile of trails circle six ponds for waterfowl from across the nation and the world—an Alaska pond, prairie pothole pond, Chesapeake pond, international pond, woodland pond, and special pond for rare dusky Canada geese. Another pond with a resident population of wood ducks, hooded mergansers, redheads, and trumpeter swans can be viewed from a gallery at the visitor's center, where related books and gifts can be purchased.

The network of trails also circles a butterfly and hummingbird garden; a meadow with a concealed viewing station for glimpses of deer, red fox, raccoon, and muskrat; an enclosed aviary; blinds for bird watchers along Lake Knapp and Marshy Creek; and a picnic area.

The Wildfowl Trust is a private, non-profit conservation organization supported by memberships and special contributions and grants. A full-time staff of ten, with help from about fifty volunteers, manages and maintains the center and conducts an excellent selection of educational programs for students from pre-school age through grade 12.

COLONIAL QUEEN ANNE'S COUNTY COURTHOUSE

Where: On Rt. 18 off of U.S. 301 in Queenstown
When: Open by request
Phone: 410-827-7646

The reopening of this simple, primitive, colonial courthouse in May 1979 was probably the highest moment in its long history, an event attended by the chief justices of both England and the United States.

The original courthouse dates back to about 1708. The local court sat here for seventy years until, at the end of the Revolutionary War, the Maryland legislature moved the seat of the growing county to the more central location at Centreville.

In the intervening years, the old brown frame section became a dwelling. A kitchen wing was added in the early nineteenth century and another wing in 1900 was used as a store. When the structure went up for sale in 1976, a Queenstown Historic Preservation Committee headed the effort to acquire it and restore the old frame courthouse section to its original appearance. The newer brick wing became the Town Office.

What followed is described in excerpts from a story in *The* (Baltimore) *Sun* by the author of this guide ...

The chief justices of England and the United States made an international event yesterday of the reopening of the original eighteenth-century Queen Anne's County Courthouse on the town square of this Eastern Shore community of fewer than 400 residents.

The Baron John Passmore Widgery, Lord Chief Justice of England, arrived at the town square at 11 a.m. in a horse-drawn landau, accompanied by Warren E. Burger, Chief Justice of the United States Supreme Court.

The British jurist outshone his American counterpart, wearing a crimson legal robe trimmed in ermine and the thick white wig of British tradition. Lord Widgery described the restored courthouse, which was the center of yesterday's celebration here, as "the stuff of democracy and of America."

QUEEN ANNE'S MUSEUM OF EASTERN SHORE LIFE

Where: At 4-H Park, off of Rt. 18 on Dulin Clark Road
When: Open summer Saturdays and Sundays, 1 p.m. to 4 p.m.; or by appointment
Phone: 410-758-0349 or 410-758-0166

Opened on August 8, 1994, this museum celebrates what the Eastern Shore is all about, at least up to now—rural life. Here are familiar items from farm and farm-home in the not too distant past, or, in some cases, the present—items such as a corn sheller, cider

Familiar but now obsolete items of farm and home make the new Queen Anne's Museum of Eastern Shore Life a feast of memories.

press, farm wagon with the harnesses for work horses, blacksmithing tools, farm kitchen with drop-leaf table and cabinet, and the oyster tongs and other waterman's gear for the traditional sideline of the Shore farm.

The exhibits are housed in a new building designed for the purpose, are well laid out, and gleam with care.

It is a museum that will undoubtedly grow with time and discovery.

"21"—THE ABSTRACT SCULPTURE AT TIDEWATER PUBLISHING CORPORATION NEAR CENTREVILLE

Where: East of Centreville on U.S. 301

This abstract sculpture called "21" is a landmark on U.S. 301 near Centreville.

The arresting twenty-one-foot-high sculpture standing before the Tidewater Corporation takes its title simply from its height. It has become a landmark to many regular travelers along a stretch of U.S. 301 where expanses of farmland and woods offer little to mark one's whereabouts.

The huge oval doughnut-like shape was done in ferroconcrete and is the natural color of the white sand aggregate.

It was designed by Margo Allmon, a sculptor who lives in West Grove, Pennsylvania. Michael Quinn, a former curator at the Easton Academy of the Arts, executed the work from Ms. Allmon's model, at a boatyard in Cambridge that was then experimenting with concrete boats.

From the top, one can actually go down inside the sculpture. It was designed, according to Arthur Kudner, Tidewater's president, to soften the hard lines of the company's new building.

CENTREVILLE

THE STATUE OF QUEEN ANNE

*Where: On the courthouse lawn at 122 N. Commerce
Street*

When the bronze statue of Queen Anne was
unveiled in June 1977, Princess Anne of England,
accompanied by her then-husband, Capt. Mark
Philips, came to this rural county seat for the ceremony. She was welcomed by Leonard E. Smith, a
country storekeeper who was then president of the
Queen Anne's County commissioners. The presence of the princess had seemed so fitting for the
occasion that they had sent her the invitation the
previous fall. "But who would have thought the
princess would come?" he said.

The unveiling revealed a seated figure of the queen
who ruled England from 1702 to 1714 when this
county was created by the General Assembly of the
Maryland province. She is seated in a Queen Anne
chair, her hand resting on a candlestand. A spaniel is
asleep under the chair.

The bronze statue of Queen Anne, unveiled by Princess Anne of England in 1977, stands in the lawn of the Queen Anne's County Courthouse which, with its white brick and window boxes, is an attraction in itself.

The statue was a Bicentennial gift to the county by a local benefactor, Arthur A. Houghton Jr., through an organization he founded called the Wye Institute. The sculptor was Elisabeth Gordon Chandler of Old Lyme, Connecticut, who worked on it for two years. She had chosen the informal pose as appropriate to the white brick courthouse, the oldest in use in the state, with its window boxes and wide tree-shaded lawn.

An unaccustomed crowd of about four thousand spectators, along with state and local political figures and reporters from across the country, crowded into this small town for the unveiling ceremony and related events. They were not disappointed. Princess Anne was everything a princess should be, arriving to a trumpet fanfare by red-coated marines, viewing a parade of Chesapeake Bay workboats at Kent Narrows from aboard the Governor's yacht, meeting guests at an evening picnic on the lawn at Wye Plantation, and attending Sunday morning services at Old Wye Church, as well as an afternoon horse show at Gunston School.

Most of the more than three hundred clippings about the event from all parts of the country quoted the same line from the Princess's remarks at the ceremony. "Queen Anne's County has found a happy medium in the rush of modern society. The people here have managed to fit into an energetic country and still have time for each other."

WRIGHT'S CHANCE

Where: At 119 South Commerce Street
When: Open by appointment
Phone: 410-643-8908 or 410-758-0843

When the weathered and decrepit hulk of this old plantation house was hauled down Centreville's main street in 1964 to its new location in the heart of town, there was an outcry. What promised then to be an eyesore only a block from the town's historic courthouse and Lawyers' Row, however, has become instead an enhancement.

The house was a gift to the Queen Anne's County Historical Society, which was able to trace its chain of title back to 1744. It was listed then as "an old dwelling."

Wright's Chance (top) and the Tucker House, opposite each other on Centreville's Commerce Street, restored and furnished by the Queen Anne's County Historical Society.

The site to which it was moved was also a gift to the society, and was part of a holding called "Chesterfield," which had passed through generations of the same family since 1700.

The historical society has restored and furnished the house as its headquarters and as a symbol of the county's heritage. The outstanding feature of the interior is the paneling at the fireplace ends of the two main rooms downstairs, also a gift to the restoration by a local resident who had bought it and removed it from the house some years before for his own use.

From this early eighteenth-century plantation house one can walk almost directly across the street to a late eighteenth-century townhouse described below.

THE TUCKER HOUSE

Where: *At 124 South Commerce Street*
When: *Open by appointment*
Phone: *410-643-8908 or 410-758-0843*

The red brick steps to the door of this modest and charming two-story townhouse rise directly from the brick sidewalk on a street that looks as much a part of the past as the house does. It is believed to be the oldest original house in Centreville and was a gift to the Queen Anne's County Historical Society.

With two houses to maintain and furnish, historical society members have been generous to both. The Tucker House contains some beautiful period pieces, genealogical records, and historic photographs and maps.

ALSO OF NOTE

ST. LUKE'S AT CHURCH HILL

Where: Off of Rt. 213 between Centreville and
Chestertown

St. Luke's observed its 250th anniversary in
1978 with a booklet on its long history by a widely
respected reporter and writer, the late Dickson
Preston. The church was completed in 1728 to
serve scattered parishioners who could reach it by
boat at the head of the southeast branch of the
Chester River. It gave the name to the village that
grew up around it, Church Hill.

Both the church and the village are worth a
stop. A restoration in 1880 gave the church the
Gothic look then preferred. In 1957 the stained
glass windows were replaced with clear glass to
return the church to its colonial appearance. Par-
ticularly striking are the warmth of the old brick,
its semi-circular apse, and gambrel roof.

The church acquired unsightly properties
around it, razed them, and in 1966 dedicated the
formal memorial garden that now sets it apart on
Main Street.

CHURCH HILL THEATRE

Where: *At 103 Walnut Street*
When: *Call for information*
Phone: *410-734-1331*

Rescued from abandonment by community activists some years ago, the old Art Deco theater has been turned into a live theater for summer stock and a variety of special performances on weekends throughout the year.

A phone call to the box office for the current schedule can be rewarding.

BRIDGETOWN CHURCH

Where: *Near Ridgely on Rt. 304*

This small brick church in its lonely location near the line between Queen Anne's and Caroline counties is the oldest building in the Peninsula Conference of the Methodist Church.

It was built in 1773 by the Church of England as a chapel and parish house. In the Revolutionary War, it was confiscated by American forces and given to the Presbyterians, who gave it in turn to the Methodists. Methodist services have been held here continuously ever since.

Methodism was just beginning to spread from England to America in this period. Itinerant Methodist preachers travelled through the colonies, organizing societies, but were not authorized to administer the sacraments until after the Revolution when the Church was officially established.

It was nearby on this peninsula, at Barratt's Chapel near Frederica, Delaware, that the Reverend Thomas Coke, newly arrived from England, met the missionary preacher, the Reverend Francis Asbury, on November 14, 1784, and planned the organization of a separate church in America. At that meeting, Reverend Coke became the first ordained Methodist minister to administer the sacrament of the Lord's Supper in America.

DUDLEY'S CHAPEL AT DUDLEY CORNERS

Where: On Rt. 300 west of Sudlersville

The simple structure of stucco-covered brick on a rural Queen Anne's County road was built in 1783 by a Society of Methodists a year before the Methodist Church was formally organized in America. The three bishops of the new Church—

Francis Asbury, Thomas Coke, and Richard Whatcoat—all preached at Dudley Chapel.

The chapel is named for the local farmer who gave the land for it. Now on the National Register of Historic Places, it is still in active use on special annual occasions.

SUDLERSVILLE TRAIN STATION MUSEUM

Where: On Rt. 300 at Linden Avenue (by the railroad)
When: Open for special events
Phone: 410-438-3501

For the traveler through this little-visited rural town, the tiny train-station museum by the rail-road is not exactly a destination, but a discovery that can give identity to a town perhaps otherwise passed through unheeded.

The little train station in Sudlersville has become not only a museum but a stimulus and center for annual community events.

The railroad where passengers once boarded trains from this station is now used irregularly only by the Southern States Grain Marketing operation nearby. When the old station went up for auction, it was bought by Elizabeth Stafford, wife of the last station master, J. Wilbur Stafford, and given to the Sudlersville Community Betterment Club, Inc. It was fixed up, painted, and dedicated as a museum in 1991.

Inside are an old luggage cart and documents and artifacts related to the late nineteenth century—when the railroad brought Sudlersville its greatest growth before or since—as well as to its favorite sons and landmark events. Its local heroes are James E. (Jimmy) Foxx, youngest player to be elected, in 1951, to the Baseball Hall of Fame; Dr. Hayden Metcalfe, first doctor on the East Coast to diagnose Rocky Mountain Spotted Fever; and Simon Newcomb, a nineteenth-century Sudlersville teacher who became a world renowned astronomer. Also honored are Elsie George Sudler, the first woman, in 1910, to receive a driver's license in Maryland; and Anna C. Harrison, who, in 1918, became the first female school principal on the Eastern Shore.

Not a bad heritage from small town America. The preservation of the little train station has brought it together and created a focal point for annual community events.

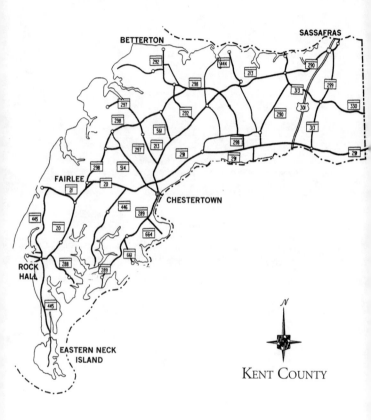

BETTERTON

SASSAFRAS

FAIRLEE

CHESTERTOWN

ROCK HALL

EASTERN NECK ISLAND

N

KENT COUNTY

KENT COUNTY

CHESTERTOWN

THE FOUNTAIN ON CHESTERTOWN'S GREEN

The marvelously ornate fountain in the heart of Chestertown's downtown was dedicated on August 19, 1899, in a ceremony that would be the envy of any small town chamber of commerce today.

Before the advent of the fountain, the Green was a rundown market center. The Ladies Improvement Society, forerunner of the Chestertown Garden Club, conceived the distinctive Green and purchased the cast-iron fountain, made of more than one hundred pieces, from Robert Wood's Ornamental Iron-Works in Philadelphia.

Chestertown's ornate fountain on The Green was dedicated in 1899 with a ceremony as splendid as the fountain itself.

Hundreds of spectators lined the streets at its dedication, an event that also featured the first automobile on the Shore south of Cecil County. It was driven from Tolchester by John H. Vandergrift.

A contest for the honor of unveiling the fountain was won by five-year-old Ida Smith who, according to accounts of the occasion, wore white Swiss cotton trimmed in Valenciennes and ribbons, white silk stockings, and white kid slippers. She was accompanied by the runner-up, Rebecca Aldrich, and six attendants.

As a silk cord was pulled, the fountain came to life with water cascading from the mouths of swans. There were bouquets in the urns. The figure on top, Hebe, goddess of youth and beauty and cupbearer to the gods, was crowned with a wreath of roses.

There was music by an orchestra and a chorus of fifty.

In a formal ceremony, the Ladies Improvement Society turned the park and the fountain over to the town commissioners.

In 1992 the Chestertown Garden Club had major repairs made to the fountain by an iron-works in Beltsville. The mayor and council added lighting and continue to maintain The Green as a setting suited to the fountain's splendor.

GEDDES-PIPER HOUSE

Where: *At Church Alley*
When: *Open May through October, Monday: 9 a.m. to 3 p.m.; Wednesday and Thursday: 9 a.m. to 11:30 a.m.; Saturday and Sunday: 1 p.m. to 4 p.m.*
Phone: *410-778-3499*

The Historical Society of Kent County acquired this early eighteenth-century brick townhouse in 1958 and restored it as a house museum and society headquarters. It is just around the corner from Lawyers' Row, a street of small one- and two-story offices beside the courthouse that appear to belong to another century, and in fact do.

The house is named for two merchants who were its earliest owners. William Geddes, the first, was customs collector of the Port of Chestertown at the time when rebellion against British domination was building toward the Revolutionary War.

He is presumed to be the owner of the brigantine *Geddes,* which, in a parallel of the Boston Tea Party, was boarded by angry Chestertown citizens in May 1774, and its boxes of tea thrown into the Chester River. (A shipment of rum, according to some accounts, was spared.)

The Tea Party is re-enacted every year on the last Saturday in May as the centerpiece of a weekend festival.

Another annual event at which this house is featured is the Chestertown Candlelight Walking Tour on the second Saturday in September. This is a very special way to see a very special town. Its many historic structures, including the wonderful row of early eighteenth-century houses facing the Chester River waterfront, are private and open only for such special events.

THE WHITE SWAN TAVERN

Where: Across from the courthouse on High Street
When: Open regularly for overnight guests and at
2 p.m. daily for tea

The simplicity of the 1790s tavern has, in the White Swan, become the elegance of the l990s.

The guest enters a wide hallway between what appear at first glance to be austere public rooms with uncarpeted wide plank floors and plain wooden tables and chairs. But it is not so simple. The original eighteenth-century woodwork—moldings, deep window-sills, and mantelpiece—has been restored with carefully researched authenticity, even to wooden pins fitting together the door and window frames.

Tea at the White Swan should be part of a visit to Chestertown.

Each of the four bedrooms upstairs is done in the style of a different period, and another in the original kitchen wing has a brick floor, original ceiling beams, and black iron cooking pots and other implements beside the fireplace.

A portion of the White Swam was built before 1733. It was enlarged in 1795. It had been owned by the same family for 120 years and its main portion was a newsstand when it was acquired by Christian and Horace Havemeyer for restoration in 1980. The new owners returned it to its original use as a tavern with a contemporary designation—"Bed and Breakfast."

The restoration began with research and an archaeological dig. In glass cases in a public room downstairs is a display of items unearthed in the dig, including part of a pottery bowl with a figure of a swan that gave the new tavern its name.

There is also a piece of black marble from the fireplace in the original tavern found to have been quarried in Kilkenny, Ireland. Matching marble for the restoration was discovered and acquired from an old house near that quarry.

The White Swan and similar restoration projects in recent years have brought in their wake new specialty shops and restaurants. The changes have enlivened the downtown, but fortunately, not yet to the point of dispelling the illusion of simpler times.

EMMANUEL CHURCH

Where: On High Street by The Green

Although not the oldest or most architecturally distinguished of the many early Episcopal churches on the Eastern Shore, Emmanuel Church has a history of special significance to this denomination.

Following the victory of the American forces in the Revolutionary War, most of the Anglican clergy had either resigned from their posts or gone to England or Canada. It was in Chestertown in

1780 that Emmanuel's rector, the Reverend Dr. William Smith, also founder of Washington College, called a conference of clergy and laymen who adopted a Book of Common Prayer and the name Protestant Episcopal Church to replace the designation Church of England in the Province.

Emmanuel Church was thus the site of actions that led to the founding of the Protestant Episcopal Church in America.

Dr. Smith, a friend of George Washington and Thomas Jefferson, is given much of the credit for reshaping the heritage of the Episcopal Church after the Revolutionary War.

The colonial brick walls of this church in the heart of Chestertown are almost obscured today by additions and modifications, but the church still reflects in its appearance a heritage that began when it was first built in 1768.

WASHINGTON COLLEGE

Washington College was founded in 1782, establishing it as the tenth-oldest chartered college in the United States and the first college of the new nation. George Washington, for whom the college was named, was an early benefactor and a member of the college's Board of Visitors and Governors un-

A highlight of Washington College's early years was a visit by George Washington in 1784, and a highlight on its campus is Lee Lawrie's statue honoring the man.

til 1789, when he became the President of the United States. The bronze statue of George Washington was the gift of sculptor Lee Lawrie, commemorating the college's 175th anniversary in 1957.

In addition to George Washington, the college has hosted visits by three United States presidents: Franklin D. Roosevelt, Harry S Truman, and Dwight D. Eisenhower.

Although there is no marker indicating it, the brick sidewalk parallel to Route 213 is an interesting footnote to American literary history. Novelist James M. Cain, whose father was president of the school, attended classes at Washington College during the time the sidewalk was being built. While watching laborers lay the bricks, he listened closely to their conversations. Cain later used their tough banter as a model for the dialogue he wrote in his famous novels, often credited with helping start the "hard-boiled" school of American fiction.

Today the college is a nationally recognized selective liberal arts institution with an enrollment of approximately one thousand students. The intimacy of a small-college environment, the tradition a challenging liberal arts curriculum, and the relaxed informality characteristic of the Chesapeake Bay region continue to exert their influence on the college and its students.

St. Paul's at Fairlee

Where: Nine miles west of Chestertown on Rt. 21

Established in 1629, St. Paul's Episcopal Church was built in 1713 and paid for in the currency of the day: seventy thousand pounds of tobacco. Some of the pews are still occupied by descendants of the original owners.

Both the church and the vestry house, which was built in 1766, were restored in the 1940s through the benevolence of Glenn L. Martin, the aircraft maker who owned a nearby estate, Remington Farms, now a federal waterfowl preserve.

Trees that predate the colony shade an extensive churchyard in which the earliest dated tombstone is October 20, 1729. The gravestone that visitors inevitably seek out, however, is that of actress Tallulah Bankhead, a frequent visitor to Kent County who chose this as her burial site.

CHESAPEAKE FARMS

Where: On Rt. 20 about 8 miles west of Chestertown
Phone: 410-778-1565

Several thousand acres of farm and woodland are managed by the corporate owner for the preservation of soil, water, and most especially, waterfowl and game. A Sanctuary Pond Drive is open all year between dawn and dusk, but is best in fall when the migrating geese and ducks fill the air with sound. A five-mile Wildlife Drive, accessed on the north side of Rt. 20, is open from February 1 to mid-October, after hunting season.

ROCK HALL

ROCK HALL MUSEUM

Where: In Rock Hall's Municipal Building on South
*   Main Street*
When: Open Wednesday through Friday, 2 p.m. to
*   4:30 p.m.; Saturday, 11 a.m. to 1 p.m.;*
*   Sunday, 2 p.m. to 4:30 p.m.*
Phone: 410-778-1399

Rock Hall is "nowhere by land," in the words of one of the town's marina owners. It is at the dead end of Rt. 20, about twelve miles west of Chestertown. Its big distinction now, as in 1707 (the year it was founded), is its location by water. The long history molded by that location is visible in the very personal, homey, and bit overcrowded town museum.

Prints and artifacts recall for the visitor the town's colonial and early American years when the now-quiet shores of Eastern Neck Island were lined with shipyards building hundreds of ocean-going sailing vessels for the young maritime nation. This was the heritage that produced a local hero of the Revolutionary War, Lambert Wickes, who commanded the ship *Reprisal* carrying the new Secretary of the Navy, Benjamin Franklin, on his diplomatic mission to France.

Rock Hall was linked to Annapolis by ferry and to Philadelphia by turnpike. Travelers passing through included George Washington, Thomas Jefferson, and James Madison. A high moment of the town's past remembered here was the passing through of Colonel Tench Tilghman, a Shore native son, on his way from Yorktown to Philadelphia to inform Congress of General Cornwallis's surrender.

ROCK HALL'S WATERMEN

Two watermen, one in wood and one in bronze, are permanent reminders of a way of life that existed in this village for over 300 years.

A larger-than-life carved wooden waterman in rain slicker and hat stands unchanging amid the changing scene around him at the juncture of Rt. 20 and Rock Hall's Main Street. Beside him stands a waterman's shanty, a symbol of his occupation.

The waterman carved of wood and standing at the entrance to Rock Hall's Main Street is an unchanging symbol of a fast changing town.

Farther into town, on the harbor, at the foot of Caroline Avenue, a more recent sixteen-foot bronze figure of a waterman tonging for oysters is a memorial to both a much respected local waterman, Stanley Vansant, and the life he represents. A workboat nearby might be unloading its catch of the day, but the dominant scene in this harbor today is marinas lined with pleasure boats.

The wooden waterman at the head of Main Street has stood there since 1973. It is the work of Jacquin Smolens, a sculptor in wood who lived and worked here until late 1988 when he moved his shop to Landenburg, Pennsylvania. Working with him was Clifton Simns, a local waterman who had taken to carving. The project was backed by the Kent County Watermen's Association and the town purchased the big tulip poplar log from which the waterman was carved.

For this and other of his big pieces, Mr. Smolens used a chain saw as a sculptor's tool. Other examples of his work will catch the eye at the Sailing Emporium, Inc. in Rock Hall, at the Georgetown Yacht Basin on the Sassafras River, and as the sign for The Granary, a restaurant on the Georgetown harbor. At the Baltimore Inner Harbor, south of the Science Center, a playground contains wooden pieces created by Mr. Smolens from trees cut down for city projects.

Recycling trees into functional sculpture is a reflection of Mr. Smolens's very personal philosophy of art: ". . . to produce beauty and utility out of nearly nothing . . ."

Behind Mr. Smolens's waterman stands a refurbished fishing shanty, a portable home that was once very much a part of the life of a Rock Hall waterman. It is a simple homemade structure once towed behind a workboat on a scow or barge to provide the waterman with a home away from home as he worked the fishing grounds up and down the bay. The shanty was refurbished and brought to this small, grassy square by "Friends of Stanley B. Vansant."

It is Mr. Vansant, a local waterman for most of his 81 years, who also represents all local watermen in the more recent bronze statue on the harbor. This is the work of Kenneth Herlihy, a retired businessman in Philadelphia who had sculpted as an avocation for many years and now does it full-time. The project was jointly financed by Mr. Herlihy and the Rock Hall Arts Council. Its unveiling on October 7, 1995, amid festivities, music, and speeches, was attended by hundreds of townspeople.

WATERMAN'S MUSEUM

Where: In Rock Hall on Rt. 20 next door to Haven Harbor Marina
When: Open year round daily from 10 a.m. to 5 p.m., except major holidays. If closed, key can be obtained at the marina.
Phone: 410-778-6697

Created in a remodeled old residence by the waterfront, this museum preserving the heritage of the local watermen opened on Memorial Day 1993.

This private venture was conceived and carried through by William T. Brawner, whose

Washington-based company owns the marina next door. He enlisted the help of Richard Burton, a company official who had retired to West Virginia but has become totally immersed in Rock Hall's heritage.

The museum features, along with watermen's tools, nets, photographs, and family albums, a re-created waterman's shanty so real it gives the visitor a start. It reflects a way of life rapidly giving way to a new era evident in the swarms of pleasure boaters who dock at the harbor on summer evenings for steamed crabs at dockside restaurants. The museum will undoubtedly grow, adding actual retired workboats to its collection outdoors.

KENT COUNTY FARM MUSEUM

Where: *On Rt. 448 near Turners Creek Public*
           Landing
When: *Open Saturday, June through October: 10 a.m.*
           to 4 p.m.; or by appointment
Phone: *410-778-3757*

When the farm museum at Turners Creek got underway in the 1970s, its initiators hoped it would be to Maryland farming what the Chesapeake Bay Maritime Museum at St. Michaels is to the lore of the bay. Although this has not yet happened, members of Kent Museum, Inc. have assured that farm machinery and tools of the past collected in the big steel shed here will not be abandoned and lost.

The museum's directors and most of its members and supporters are working farmers. An old-time Threshing Day Dinner at Turners Creek Landing every August raises money for the museum's maintenance and survival.

Housed in the shed are such items as a combine, a roll baler, tomato transplanter, and silo filler. Of special interest is an old horse-drawn Schauber corn-cutter, invented and manufactured in Chestertown, that was one step removed from hand harvesting.

Most of the equipment here dates from the period when farmers were changing from work horses and mules to tractors—a period in the memory of anyone over sixty who was reared on a farm.

The spirit that was behind this isolated museum at its start is still alive. Whether or not it attracts outsiders in significant numbers, the museum embodies a sense of community in one of the state's most beautiful farming areas.

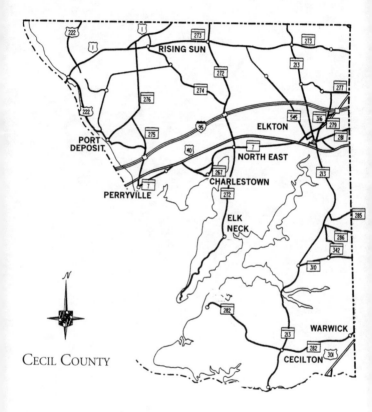

CECIL COUNTY

CECIL COUNTY

Cecil County, at the head of the bay, has a split personality, at least as seen by the outside world.

In its southern half, below the Chesapeake and Delaware Canal, it is estate and farm country that is definitely Eastern Shore in character. Its northern half, however, is crossed by U.S. 1, U.S. 40, and Interstate 95 and runs into Delaware on one edge and Pennsylvania on the other. It seems to belong to the metropolitan Western Shore.

Sometimes it is listed as an Eastern Shore county and sometimes as Central Maryland. Whatever its designation, it is a link between the two distinct segments of Maryland separated geographically, culturally, and politically by the Chesapeake Bay. It is the only way to get from one to the other without crossing the bay. The connection between Cecil and the rest of the state is simply the bridge across the Susquehanna at Havre de Grace.

OLD BOHEMIA, ST. FRANCIS XAVIER JESUIT MISSION

Where: *Two miles north of Warwick. Reached by Rt. 282 from Rt. 213 (look for historic marker) or by Rt. 299 from U.S. 13.*
When: *Open annually on the third Sundays of April, May, September, and October from 1 p.m. to 6 p.m.*
Phone: *410-275-2866*

Whether or not the church is open, this site is worth a detour simply to connect with its remarkable history and the recent restoration effort.

The original portion of St. Francis Xavier Church dates to 1793. It was part of a Jesuit plantation established in 1704 in what was then a wilderness. It was one of the earliest permanent bases of the Catholic Church in the English colonies.

The most significant contribution of the Bohemia mission to the New World was an academy that was started there in 1741. The children of wealthy Catholic families in Maryland were sent there for their schooling, most notably two cousins, John and Charles Carroll.

In 1789 John Carroll, one of the academy's first students, became the founder of Georgetown University, the nation's oldest Catholic university. He also became the nation's first Catholic bishop and later archbishop of Baltimore.

Charles Carroll of Carrollton was a Maryland signer of the Declaration of Independence.

The original mission farm had been sold to a local farmer and the church was deteriorating when the Old Bohemia Historical Society, Inc. was organized in 1953 to restore and preserve it as a Catholic shrine.

The church is surrounded by 3.8 acres of lawn and cemetery. In a bower of boxwood are ten graves of the Jesuit priests who left Europe and established the original mission.

Artifacts unearthed in the restoration process are on display in a house connected to

Old Bohemia, St. Francis Xavier Jesuit Mission, seems almost as lonely to today's visitor as when it was part of a Jesuit plantation established in what was then a wilderness in 1704.

the north side of the church that dates from about
1825.

The shrine is under the jurisdiction of the
Wilmington Diocese.

C & D CANAL MUSEUM IN CHESAPEAKE CITY

Where: *On the canal at Second Street and Bethel Road*
When: *Open daily from 8 a.m. to 4:15 p.m.;*
Sunday from 10 a.m. to 6 p.m.
Phone: *410-885-5621*

The climactic exhibit at this National Register site is the huge cypress wood and iron
waterwheel which lifted water into the Chesapeake and Delaware Canal from 1856 to 1927.
It is preserved in the original wheel house. It is
thirty-eight feet in diameter and ten feet wide.
As a steam engine turned the wheel, its twelve
huge buckets once lifted 170 tons of water a
minute from a deep well into an upper race or
channel that carried it into the canal lock at
Chesapeake City. As the wheel lifted water into
the lock, a vessel was lifted sixteen feet above
the level of the creek.

The canal wheel at Chesapeake City was famous in its day. It was conceived by two engineers
from Philadelphia in response to a competition

announced by the canal company for the best plan for raising the water level in the canal.

The pumphouse was designated a National Historic Landmark in 1965. The museum of which it is a part is operated by the United States Army Corps of Engineers.

When the canal opened in 1829, it was a landmark in American technology. By connecting the Delaware and Chesapeake Bays, it reduced by three hundred miles the distance a boat would have to travel between Baltimore and Philadelphia and cut equally significant mileage from Baltimore to New York and European ports.

The canal was financed by stockholders in the Chesapeake and Delaware Canal Company incorporated in 1799 by the legislatures of Maryland, Pennsylvania, and Delaware. Boats paid tolls to go through.

Traffic was heavy from the start. There were coal and lumber barges towed first by mules and later by tugs. Showboats and floating stores visited the canal towns.

In 1919 the canal was bought by the United States government and has been operated since by the Corps of Engineers. Since 1927 it has been a sea level canal with no tolls, no locks, and no need for the big lift wheel.

To handle today's waterborne commerce, the canal's width has been increased to 450 and its depth to 35 feet. With more than 22,000 vessels using it every year, it is said to be one of the busiest waterways in the world.

The canal museum traces its history with films, photographs, and models.

Chesapeake City is itself an inviting destination. The ferry that once carried cars across the canal here was replaced in 1949 by a lofty fixed bridge carrying Rt. 213 traffic high over the rooftops of the town. The town has blossomed in recent years with restored houses, bed and breakfasts, and restaurants.

Sitting at a canal-side restaurant at Chesapeake City, on open decks in summer, a diner can watch ocean-going freighters dwarf the many pleasure boats that share the waterway with them.

SINKING SPRINGS HERB FARM

Where: *On Elk Forest Road about 2 miles west off Rt. 213 just north of the C & D Canal bridge at Chesapeake City*
When: *Open daily 9 a.m. to 4 p.m.; closed Sunday*
Phone: *410-398-5566*

The visitor here is transported to another world, not only by the 1712 farmhouse and rustic out-

buildings, but by the aroma of herbs growing outdoors and drying in the barn. By their presence in
literature from the most ancient of times, and
through all the senses, herbs create a continuity of
the present and the past.

Ann Stubbs is a former schoolteacher who
stopped work to rear her children and became in-
volved with herbs and dried flower arrangements.
Bill Stubbs is a history teacher whose own family
history goes back to the colonial settlement of Cecil
County. The herb farm is on property originally
granted to his family by Lord Baltimore. The farm,
which is his project, started with parsley, sage, rose-
mary, and thyme, like an echo of the folksong,
and now has over a hundred kinds of herbs.

The Stubbs family moved to this property from
another just a few years ago. In the course of repairs to the old log house, Bill Stubbs found under the weatherboards traces of the original beaded
cypress wood siding. He has since redone the whole
exterior with restoration siding bleached to a
weathered grey to match the original.

The scene is enhanced by a 417-year-old sy-
camore in the front yard listed by the state as a
Champion Tree.

Sinking Springs invites private groups or tours
for luncheons, talks, and demonstrations on the
lore of herbs and a shop, or Mux'n Room (the

term is from Shakespeare), offers for sale dried flowers, herbal teas, vinegars, potpourris, and plants.

There is a garden cottage that looks like a storybook illustration for overnight bed and breakfast visitors.

CECIL COUNTY HISTORICAL SOCIETY MUSEUM AND JOHN F. DEWITT MILITARY MUSEUM

Where: At 135 E. Main Street in Elkton
When: Open Monday, noon to 4 p.m.; Tuesday, 6 to
*   8:30 p.m.;*
Thursday, 10 a.m. to 4 p.m.; and the 4th Saturday of
*   each month, 10 a.m. to 2 p.m.*
Phone: 410-398-1790
and . . . Entry fee

Cecil County's Historical Society shares what was once a spacious Elkton home with the local Chamber of Commerce. Its collection of artifacts can thus be displayed in rooms recreating an early American kitchen; the old Taylor's Country Store near Perryville complete with counter, stocked display cases, and post office boxes; and a children's room on the upstairs gallery. There is a research library for historians and genealogists.

A separate museum within a museum displays prime items from the remarkable collection of the late Sheriff John F. DeWitt of military memorabilia from the American Revolution through the Civil War, World Wars I and II, and up to Desert Storm. The collection includes weapons, helmets, and uniforms from all sides of the conflicts and was donated to the society by heirs of the collector.

The little log building in the backyard of the house is a school started by the Reverend William Dukes in 1799. It was the county's first schoolhouse and was moved to its present site for preservation.

HISTORIC LITTLE WEDDING CHAPEL

Where: At 142 East Main Street in Elkton
When: Open Monday through Friday, 9 a.m. to 8
p.m.; Saturday, 9 a.m. to 7 p.m.; and Sunday,
10 a.m. to 4 p.m.

The little chapel, easily identified by its stone facade, is not simply a relic from the days when quickie marriages were to Elkton what casinos are to Las Vegas. It is for real. Even though Maryland law today requires a forty-eight-hour waiting period between marriage license and ceremony, an average of fifteen marriages a week are performed in this tiny chapel bedecked with artificial flowers.

Weddings are performed here for prices that vary according to the day and hour, with an additional $25 for the minister's fee. For their fee, couples receive, in addition to the ceremony, "a complimentary video, a decorative wedding certificate suitable for framing, and a wallet-size license."

One reason given for the chapel's popularity is its closeness to the Delaware and Pennsylvania borders and the fact that Maryland law does not require a blood test.

The little chapel is a survivor from the days, early in this century, when marriage was a big business in Elkton and its Main Street was lined with signs advertising "Minister, Marriage License." It is said to have begun on May 1, 1913, when Delaware passed a new marriage law establishing a waiting period for marriages. Elkton, right across the border, became almost overnight a mecca for elopers. Among the celebrities who were married here were Babe Ruth, Joan Fontaine, and John and Martha Mitchell.

In an election in 1938, Maryland voters approved the forty-eight-hour waiting period before a marriage and the boom subsided. (Cecil County voters did not approve the new law.) Nonetheless,

Elkton's identity with romance and elopement seems to linger in the town's mystique and in this little chapel.

UPPER BAY MUSEUM IN NORTH EAST

Where: Follow Rt. 272, 1 mile south of its intersection with U.S. 40. Turn right on Walnut Street to the North East Community Park.

When: Open from Memorial Day to Labor Day, Saturday and Sunday: 10 a.m. to 4 p.m.

Phone: 410-287-0672 or 287-5909

The special appeal of this museum at the head of Chesapeake Bay is contained in the simple comment of a one-time hunter and fisherman who was one of its creators: "My people used this equipment."

It was created and is operated by members of the Cecil-Harford Hunters Association. Many of them grew up in families in which hunting and fishing was a livelihood, or at least a part-time one.

They have a personal connection with watermen who fished in the Susquehanna Flats off large log floats or hauled in herring in seine nets, propelling heavily laden scows over rocky bottoms with fourteen-foot oars. Oars are heavily featured in this museum with over fifty on display, many identified by the names of the men who owned them.

There are ice poles, ice saws, and dip nets used by the mid-winter fisherman; a rail bird skiff; market guns no longer legal; gunning lights; and boat tools. There are decoys in the style of the upper bay, carved to roll with the waves in the shallows. A separate building houses a collection of antique marine engines kept up by Boy Scouts working on merit badge requirements.

The museum was the outgrowth of a decoy show the founding organization sponsored in 1967. It is on a town-owned site once owned by the old Harvey Fish Company. What was once a deserted plant building has been refurbished with the help of a state grant, and the museum seems well on the way to the wide identity it deserves.

DAY BASKET FACTORY

Where: At 110 West High Street, North East
When: Open Monday through Friday, 8:30 a.m.
to 4 p.m.; Saturday, 10 a.m. to 4 p.m.
Phone: 410-287-6100

Baskets have been made here since 1875, when the Day family started their factory. Oak baskets and pottery are for sale. Visitors can watch oak baskets being made by hand with equipment used since the factory began. The pliable oak strips from which they are made are for sale for visitors who want to try their own hand at it.

TURKEY POINT LIGHTHOUSE IN ELK NECK STATE PARK

Where: *At the end of a mile-long foot trail which begins at the dead end of Rt. 272*
Phone: *410-287-5333*

The old Turkey Point Lighthouse today sends its automatic beam across Chesapeake Bay from atop a one-hundred-foot bluff at the tip of a long peninsula containing Elk Neck State Forest and Park. Until 1947 the lighthouse was tended by the late Fannie Salter, a widow who had come there with her husband in 1922. The lightkeeper's house is now gone.

The walk to Turkey Point Lighthouse is alone worth the effort.

The lighthouse is a dramatic destination for an easy and equally dramatic walk (two miles there and back). It begins along bluffs looking out across the bay toward the North East River, Perry Point, and Havre de Grace. It continues into woods entangled with grapevines, across an open field and into more woods, opening out abruptly to the bluff and the lighthouse with a sweeping view of the bay on three sides.

There are other scenic trails in the park, wooded or marshy and teeming with birds and wildlife. Maps of the trail system can be had at the park entrance.

TORY HOUSE AND COLONIAL CHARLESTOWN

Where: *At Market and Cecil Streets. Charlestown is on Rt. 267, which turns off of Rt. 7 between North East and Perryville*
When: *Open May through October on the third Sunday each month, 2 p.m. to 4 p.m.*
Phone: *410-287-8793*

The "before and after" pictures on display in the hallway of Charlestown's eighteenth-century Tory House are a vivid reminder of the imagination and tenacity behind a restoration project such as this one. When Colonial Charlestown, Inc. acquired the house in 1974 and set out to restore it, it had been occupied by renters who had twenty-three dogs and a goat. The first step was plain old scrubbing.

The Tory House dates back to 1750. Its name came from the supposed political sympathies of its owners at the time of the Revolutionary War, a supposition that proved to be untrue, but the name has stuck anyway.

Tory House has stood in Charlestown since 1750 and its restoration has revived awareness of the town's colonial heritage.

The most interesting part of the house is the basement. It was once a tavern, and the brickwork, fireplace with crane, round brick walls of an indoor well, and donated artifacts and furnishings have revived the feel of that past role.

Charlestown, at the head of the Northeast River, was established by an Act of Assembly in September 1742, and named for Charles Calvert, the fifth Lord Baron of Baltimore. The reason for its existence was the public wharf built to encourage trade and navigation in newly developing Cecil County.

In the Revolutionary War the town became a supply depot for the Continental Army, and George Washington recorded several visits there in his diary.

To help pay for the restoration, Colonial Charlestown has revived the annual fairs where merchants in the eighteenth century brought their wares by horseback or ship.

Since the renewed awareness of the town's colonial heritage, several historic houses have been privately restored. If Tory House isn't open, Charlestown itself, one of the least known of Maryland's National Register historic places, is worth a detour off Interstate 95 or U.S. 40.

RODGERS TAVERN

Where: *On Rt. 7 in Perryville near the entrance to the VA Medical Center at Perry Point*
When: *Open May through October every second Sunday from 2 p.m. to 4 p.m.*

Rodgers Tavern

This restored eighteenth-century tavern, built of the grey granite native to this area, was a stopping place for George Washington, Thomas Jefferson, and other founding fathers as they crossed the

Susquehanna going to and from Baltimore and Philadelphia.

PORT DEPOSIT AND THE SUSQUEHANNA RIVER GREENWAY

Where: *North of Interstate 95 and south of U.S. 1 on Rt. 222*
Phone: *For Greenway information, call 410-974-3589*

Port Deposit's distinction today is a pervasive revitalization visible everywhere, from hanging flower baskets on private porches to new public streets and sidewalks. The town has always been distinctive for its buildings and homes of native grey granite, as if they had emerged from the steep granite cliffs behind them. Its Main Street stretches between the cliffs and the Susquehanna River with only a couple of side streets climbing sharply upward and ending abruptly.

Early in the last century a barge canal brought grain and coal from Pennsylvania for shipment from the town's then thriving port. Other river-related industries have come and gone. Its industrial waterfront today is the site of a new condominium development.

High above the town, Tome School, named for Jacob Tome, a local benefactor, was founded early in the nineteenth century and offered a private school education to boys—and later to girls as well—for over a century. Its grey granite buildings are now empty and awaiting a new use.

Also awaiting new development above the town is the site of the Bainbridge Naval Base through which thousands of young recruits came and went during World War II and danced on Saturday nights in its huge recreation hall to the music of big bands with busloads of local hostesses. The hall and the rest of the base's buildings have been demolished and the town looks toward a future use for the property that will enhance its new life.

For many visitors the most exciting new development to affect this town will be the Lower Susquehanna Heritage Greenway Trail. This future hiker-biker trail system will pass through Port Deposit and the town has acquired several properties to tie in with it. The Greenway is a project of the Maryland Greenways Commission within the Department of Natural Resources. There will be corridors of protected open space on both sides of the river with extensive trails eagerly awaited by those who enjoy the woods, shorelines, and vistas along the Susquehanna.

PAW PAW HOUSE

Where: *On Port Deposit's Main Street*
When: *Open May through October the second and*
fourth Sundays of the month from 1 p.m.
to 5 p.m.
Phone: *410-378-3236 or 378-2121*

A museum devoted to the varied and colorful heritage of Port Deposit has developed from the overall revitalization of the town and is part of the new look of its Main Street, strung along the Susquehanna.

PLUMPTON PARK ZOOLOGICAL GARDENS

Where: *On Rt. 272 3½ miles east of Rising Sun*
Phone: *410-658-6850*
and . . . Entry fee

To the visitor, Plumpton Park has the informal, unpolished look of an ordinary barnyard, except that the animals and birds in their tree-shaded pens and fenced pastures are camels, zebras, a South African gemsbok, gazelle, elands, emus, rheas, ostriches, and Australian black swans. There are Watusi cattle with enormous horns and a field of American bison. There are a pair of gentle and appealing lemurs, a threatened mammal now confined mainly to Madagascar.

Children are especially attracted to the sizable herd of small white, chocolate, and spotted fallow deer with their broad antlers, another threatened species. A wild boar snores loudly in his pen. Peacocks move freely about, and a visitor can find himself staring eye to eye at an owl in his cage.

There is an intimacy about this zoo that gives it a special appeal. It began as the private collection of Ed Plumstead and just kept growing until it was opened to the public in 1986. He knows the animals (over three hundred of them) personally and regular visitors feel they do too.

In this era of cutbacks in government spending, a Cecil County subsidy has ended and the zoo is supported by admission fees, donations, fund-raising events, and volunteer help.

FAIR HILL NATURAL RESOURCES AREA

Where: *Near the juncture of Rts. 213 and 273, north of Elkton*
When: *Natural area open from dawn to dusk.*
Phone: *410-398-4909 or 398-1246*

Fair Hill's 5,613 acres of farmland, woods, and marsh offer a mix of uses from a race track with pari-mutuel betting to miles of wooded trails where a hiker or mountain biker can be completely alone.

For some it is essentially an equestrian center, with a three-hundred-acre Training Center for race horses; a turf course for steeplechase and flat races; competitions in dressage, cross country, and stadium jumping; and a carriage driving championship that is part of an International Three-Day Event the last weekend in October. (For International tickets, call 410-885-2523. For information on the Spring Steeplechase Races, call 410-398-6565.)

For hundreds of local school children and summer day campers, Fair Hill means the Nature and Environmental Center. Its headquarters is a former du Pont hunting lodge in the natural resources area, overlooking a freshwater marsh maintained by local, federal, and private conservation organizations.

For the visitor simply looking for open space, there is access from the parking area near the center to trails for biking, hiking, or fishing along Big Elk Creek. Crossing the creek is one of Cecil County's two remaining covered bridges, this a reconstructed, red, and very photogenic one.

To reach the natural area, turn off Rt. 273 just east of its intersection with Rt. 213. Although the dirt road off the highway is not well marked, it is in sight of the grandstands at the race track and fair grounds. After entering the Fair Hill property from Rt. 273, keep bearing to the left, crossing the highway on an overhead bridge. The roadway winds through woods and farm fields. Follow the signs marked FHNEC (Fair Hill Nature and Environmental Center).

The road passes through extensive hayfields that not only feed about four hundred horses that are usually at the training center here, but provide revenue for maintaining this vast tract.

At the western edge of the Natural Resources area, Fair Hill Inn is convenient for hikers, bikers, or fishermen who like to combine gourmet eating with rustic activity.

National and State Parks

NATIONAL PARKS

Assateague Island National Seashore (Worcester County) A thirty-seven-mile-long barrier island with beach and campsites reached from the north end by Rt. 611 off of U.S. 50 south of Ocean City, and beaches that can be reached from the south, or Virginia end, by turning off of U.S. 50 onto Rt. 175 and crossing Chincoteague Island. Phone: 410-641-1441.

Blackwater National Wildlife Refuge (Dorchester County) Best visited in November or December when the migrating Canada geese are at their peak. Reached by turning south onto Rt. 16 just past Cambridge, then south again at Church Creek onto Rt. 335 and following signs. Phone: 410-228-2677.

Eastern Neck Island National Wildlife Refuge (Kent County) Observation stations reward the visitor with vistas for observing marsh and water birds, especially, if one is lucky, migrating swans in the fall. Phone: 410-639-7056

STATE PARKS

Assateague State Park (Worcester County) A park within a park at the north end of the National Seashore, this one has two miles of ocean beach, campsites, bath houses, bike and hike trails, canoe rentals on the bayside, and picnic tables. Phone: 410-641-2120.

Pocomoke River State Park (Worcester County) This is actually two parks, one on each side of this designated Wild and Scenic River. Milburn Landing on the north side has camp sites, fishing pier, small boat launch, picnic tables and shelter, playground, and a trail through the woods and cypress swamp that is especially awesome in the spring when the rhododendron are in bloom. Reached by turning west off of Rt. 12 toward Snow Hill, onto Rt. 354. Shad Landing, on the south side of the river, has small boat docks, canoe rentals, a swimming pool, snack bar, and camp store, in addition to campsites and picnic tables. Reached from U.S. 113 south of Snow Hill. Phone: 410-632-2566.

Janes Island State Park (Somerset County) With miles of isolated shoreline and marsh on Chesapeake Bay, an island portion that can be reached only by boat, and proximity to Crisfield, the Crab Capital of the World, campers here are really immersed in the mystique of the Eastern Shore. There are canoe rentals, camp store, boat launch, and picnic area. The park is reached by turning off of U.S. 13 onto Rt. 413 toward Crisfield, continuing for about twelve miles and turning right onto Plantation Road. Phone: 410-968-1565.

Martinak State Park (Caroline County) Quiet, wooded campsites along the Choptank River are especially favored by small boaters, fishermen, and seekers of solitude. There are a boat launch, boat rentals, hiking trails, and picnic tables. Park is reached by turning west off of Rt. 404 about two miles south of Denton. Phone: 410-479-1619.

Tuckahoe State Park (Caroline and Queen Anne's Counties) Hidden along the upper reaches of Tuckahoe Creek are about 3,500 acres of wooded marshes for hunters in season, a 20-acre lake with boat launch and rentals for fishermen, and a creek that is great for canoeing. Within the park are the trails and plantings of Adkins Arboretum. Reached off of Rt. 404 by Rt. 480 north between the towns of Queen Anne and Hillsboro. Phone: 410-634-2810.

Elk Neck State Park (Cecil County) From sandy beach and marshes to woods and high bluffs over-looking the North East River, campers and hikers have plenty of diversion. There are boat launch and rentals, fishing, picnicking, and even cross-country skiing. Reached off of U.S. 40 about nine miles south of North East on Rt. 272. Phone: 410-287-5333.

FOR FURTHER INFORMATION

Caroline County Commissioners
P.O. Box 201
Denton, MD 21629
410-479-4188

Cecil County Chamber of Commerce, Department
   of Tourism
135 E. Main Street
Elkton, MD 21921
1-800-CECIL-95

Dorchester County Tourism Office
203 Sunburst Highway
Cambridge, MD 21613
410-228-1000 or 1-800-522-TOUR

Kent County Chamber of Commerce
400 S. Cross Street
P.O. Box 146
Chestertown, MD 21620
410-778-0416

Queen Anne's County Office of Tourism
Kent Narrows Center
3100 Main Street
Grasonville, MD 21638
410-827-4810

Somerset County Tourism Office
Information Center on U.S. 50
P.O. Box 243
Princess Anne, MD 21853
410-651-2968 or 1-800-521-9189

Crisfield Area Chamber of Commerce
1-800-782-3913

Tawes Museum and Visitors Center
410-968-2501

Talbot County Conference and Visitors Bureau
P.O. Box 1366
Chamber Blvd.
Easton, MD 21601
410-822-4606

Wicomico County Convention and Visitors Bureau
Wicomico Youth and Civic Center
500 Glen Avenue
Salisbury, MD 21801
410-548-4914 or 1-800-332-8687

Worcester County Tourist Office
105 Pearl Street
P.O. Box 208
Snow Hill, MD 21863
410-632-3617

Ocean City Convention and Visitors Bureau
Ocean City Convention Hall
39th Street, 4001 Coastal Hwy.
Ocean City, MD 21842
410-289-8181

Ocean City Public Relations Department
P.O. Box 158
Ocean City, MD 21842
410-289-2800

Site Index

COLOPHON

This book was set in Adobe Garamond and CG Coronet.

Text & cover design by Diane Landskroener

Cover art by Sihn Ja An

Full page section photographs by Gibson B. Anthony

Thumbnail photographs by William J. Hingst & Mary U. Corddry

County maps by Maryland Department of Transportation,
State Highway Administration

Printed & bound by Victor Graphics, Baltimore, Maryland

The Literary House Press at Washington College wishes to thank
Kristin Callahan, Carol Casey, Meredith Davies Hadaway,
and Maureen Jacoby.